Harcourt Language

Teacher's Resource Book

Kindergarten

Harcourt
Orlando Boston Dallas Chicago San Diego

Visit *The Learning Site!*
www.harcourtschool.com

Printed in the United States of America

ISBN 0-15-317982-1

2 3 4 5 6 7 8 9 10 018 2003 2002 2001

My Alphabet Journal

by ____________________

Directions: Have children write their name on the cover of their Alphabet Journal.

Name ________________

Aa

A A

a a

Directions: Help children name the letter and the picture. Have them draw pictures whose names begin with the /a/ sound. Then trace and write the letter Aa.

Name

Bb

B B

b b

Directions: Help children name the letter and the picture. Have them draw pictures whose names begin with the /b/ sound. Then trace and write the letter Bb.

Name

Cc

Cc

Cc

Directions: Help children name the letter and the picture. Have them draw pictures whose names begin with the /k/ sound. Then trace and write the letter Cc.

Name ____________

Dd

D D

d d

Directions: Help children name the letter and the picture. Have them draw pictures whose names begin with the /d/ sound. Then trace and write the letter Dd.

Name

Ee

Ee

ee

Directions: Help children name the letter and the picture. Have them draw pictures whose names begin with the /e/ sound. Then trace and write the letter Ee.

Name ____________

Ff

Directions: Help children name the letter and the picture. Have them draw pictures whose names begin with the /f/ sound. Then trace and write the letter Ff.

Name

Gg

Gg

Directions: Help children name the letter and the picture. Have them draw pictures whose names begin with the /g/ sound. Then trace and write the letter Gg.

Name

Hh

Directions: Help children name the letter and the picture. Have them draw pictures whose names begin with the /h/ sound. Then trace and write the letter Hh.

Name ____________________

I i

Directions: Help children name the letter and the picture. Have them draw pictures whose names begin with the /i/ sound. Then trace and write the letter Ii.

Name ______________________

Jj

J J

j j

Directions: Help children name the letter and the picture. Have them draw pictures whose names begin with the /j/ sound. Then trace and write the letter Jj.

Name

Kk

Kk

Kk

Directions: Help children name the letter and the picture. Have them draw pictures whose names begin with the /k/ sound. Then trace and write the letter Kk.

Name

Directions: Help children name the letter and the picture. Have them draw pictures whose names begin with the /l/ sound. Then trace and write the letter Ll.

Name

Mm

MM

mm

Directions: Help children name the letter and the picture. Have them draw pictures whose names begin with the /m/ sound. Then trace and write the letter Mm.

Name

Nn

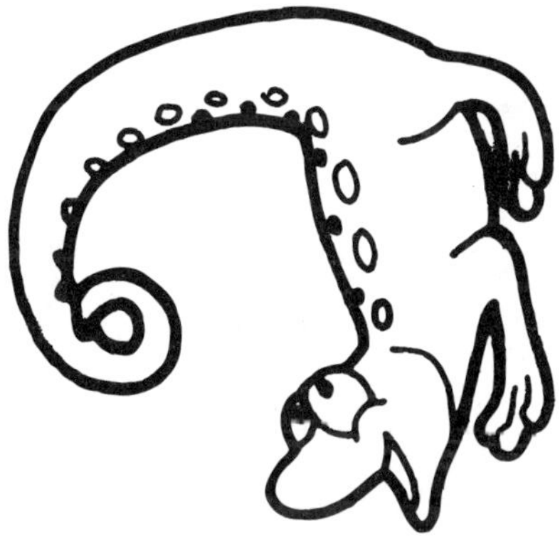

Nn

nn

Directions: Help children name the letter and the picture. Have them draw pictures whose names begin with the /n/ sound. Then trace and write the letter Nn.

Name

Oo

Directions: Help children name the letter and the picture. Have them draw pictures whose names begin with the /o/ sound. Then trace and write the letter Oo.

Name

Pp

Pp

pp

Directions: Help children name the letter and the picture. Have them draw pictures whose names begin with the /p/ sound. Then trace and write the letter Pp.

Name ____________

Qq

Qq qq

Directions: Help children name the letter and the picture. Have them draw pictures whose names begin with the /kw/ sound. Then trace and write the letter Qq.

Name

Rr

R R

r r

Directions: Help children name the letter and the picture. Have them draw pictures whose names begin with the /r/ sound. Then trace and write the letter Rr.

Name

Ss

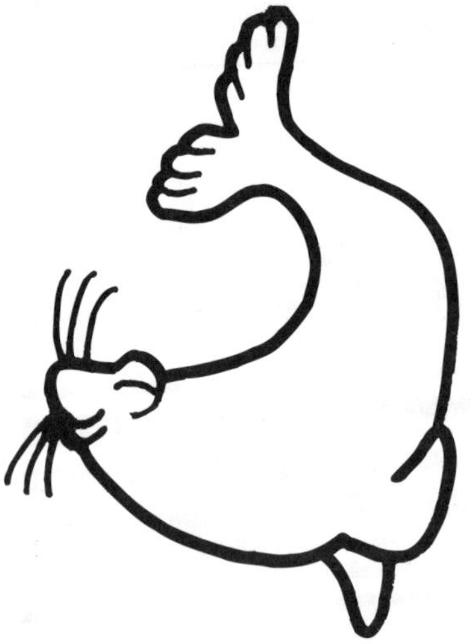

S s

s s

Directions: Help children name the letter and the picture. Have them draw pictures whose names begin with the /s/ sound. Then trace and write the letter Ss.

Name ___________

T t

Directions: Help children name the letter and the picture. Have them draw pictures whose names begin with the /t/ sound. Then trace and write the letter Tt.

Name ____________

Uu

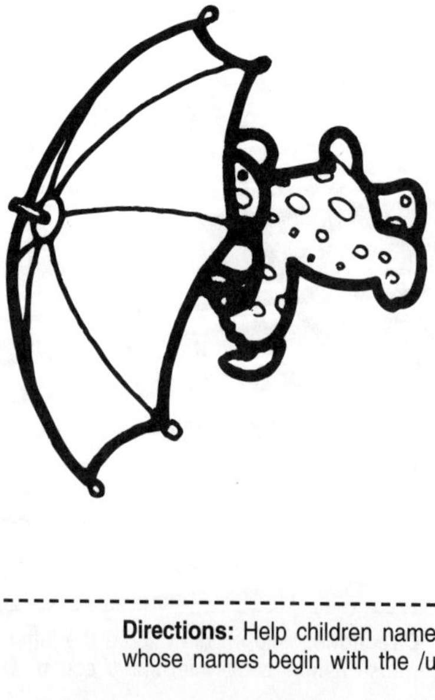

UU

uu

Directions: Help children name the letter and the picture. Have them draw pictures whose names begin with the /u/ sound. Then trace and write the letter Uu.

Name ____________

Vv

Directions: Help children name the letter and the picture. Have them draw pictures whose names begin with the /v/ sound. Then trace and write the letter Vv.

Name ______

Ww

Ww

Ww

Directions: Help children name the letter and the picture. Have them draw pictures whose names begin with the /w/ sound. Then trace and write the letter Ww.

Name ________

Xx

Directions: Help children name the letter and the picture. Have them draw pictures whose names begin with the /ks/ sound. Then trace and write the letter Xx.

Name ____________________

Y y

Directions: Help children name the letter and the picture. Have them draw pictures whose names begin with the /y/ sound. Then trace and write the letter Yy.

Name

Z z

Directions: Help children name the letter and the picture. Have them draw pictures whose names begin with the /z/ sound. Then trace and write the letter Zz.

Name ______________________________

Matching Cards

Name ______________________________

Letter Collage

Name ______________________________

Morning Message

____

____________'s Morning Message

Today is

The weather is

We will

Name ____________________

The Rhyming Wheel

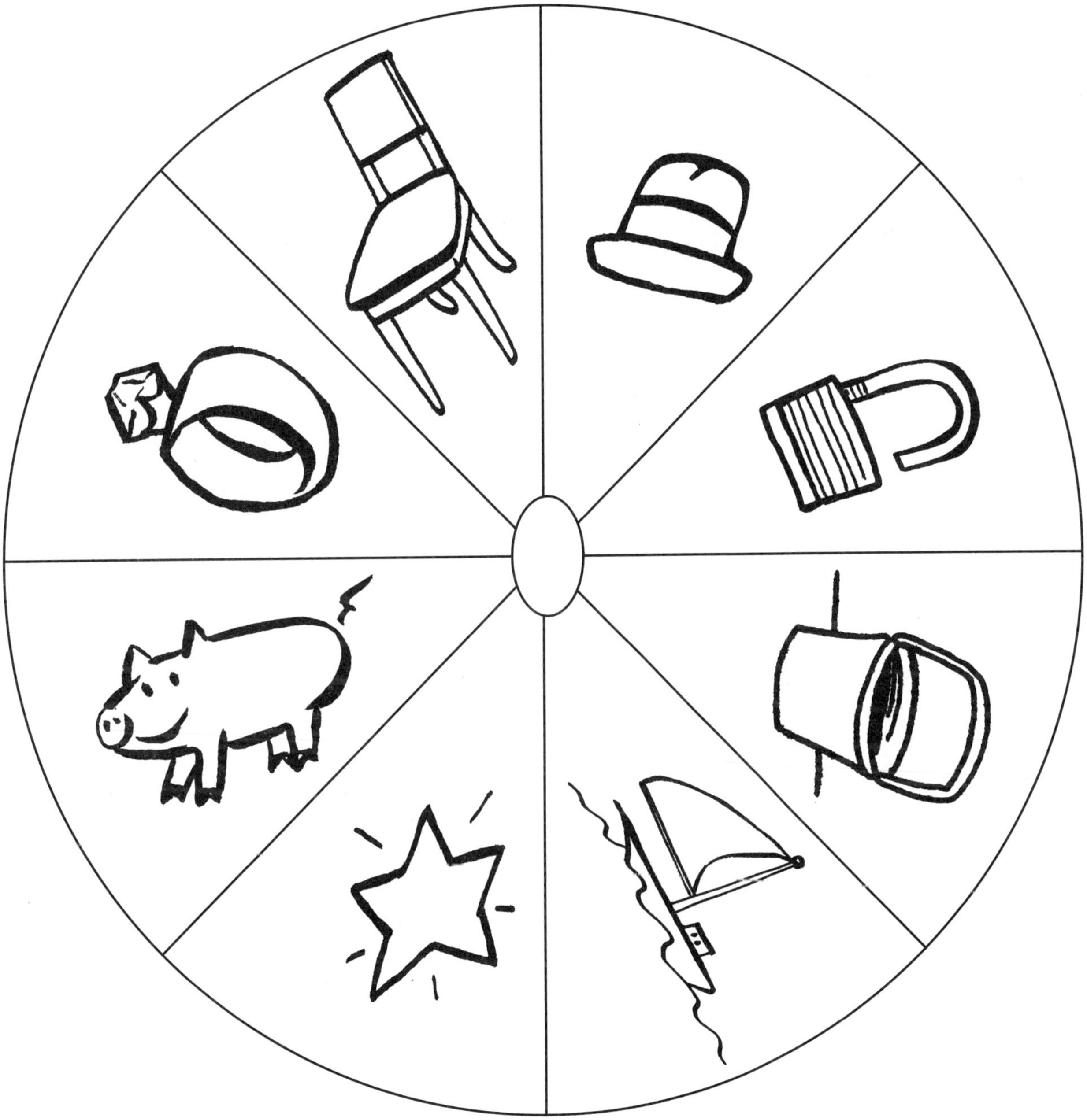

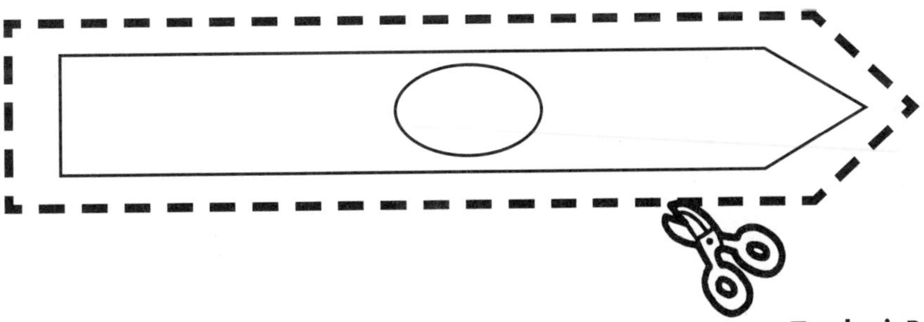

Name ______________________________

Naming Words

Name ______________________________

My Favorite Place in My Neighborhood

My favorite place in my neighborhood is

______________________________.

Name ______________________________

One and More than One

Name ____________________

It's My Birthday

My birthday is in ____________________.

Have children draw the number of candles that they will need on their next birthday on the top of the cake. Then have them write their birthday month to complete the sentence.

Name ______________________________

My Favorite Indoor Activity

I like to ______________________________ .

Name ______________________________

Action Word Cards

Name ______________________________

Neighborhood Helpers

A ______________________ is a helper in my neighborhood.

Have children identify and name the neighborhood people in the picture. Then have them color the picture and complete the sentence.

Name ______________________________

I Can . . .

I can ______________ like a ________________.

Name ______________________________

Shapes

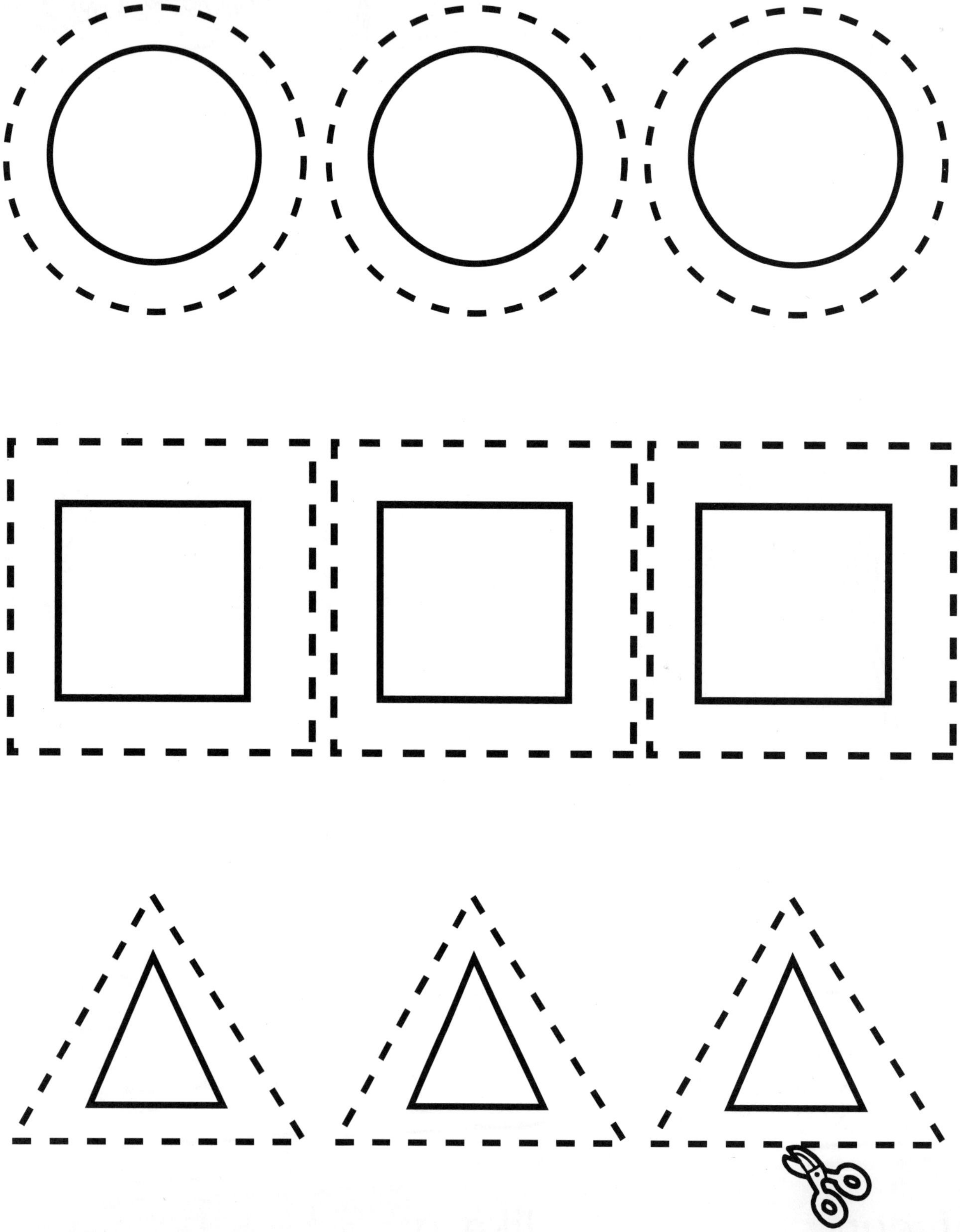

Name ______________________________

Matching Cards

6 six	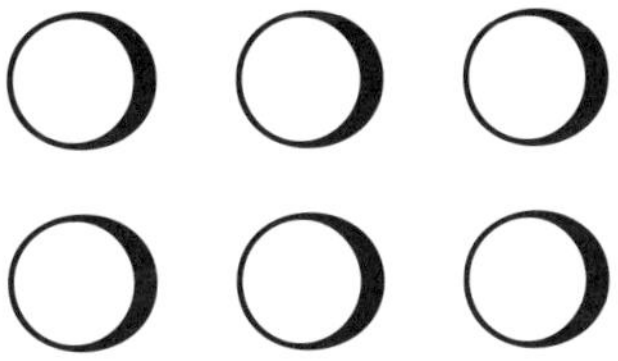
7 seven	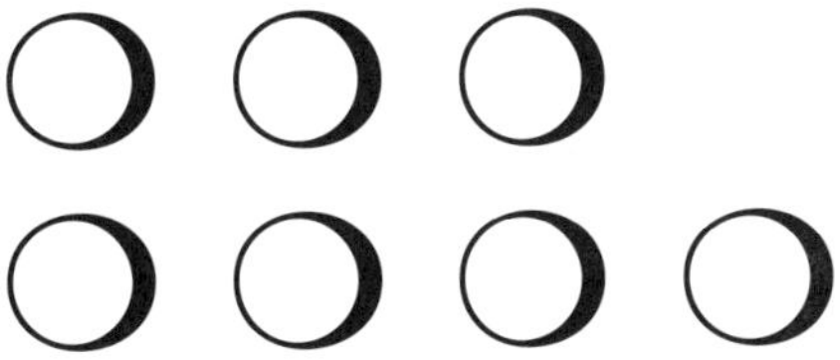
8 eight	
9 nine	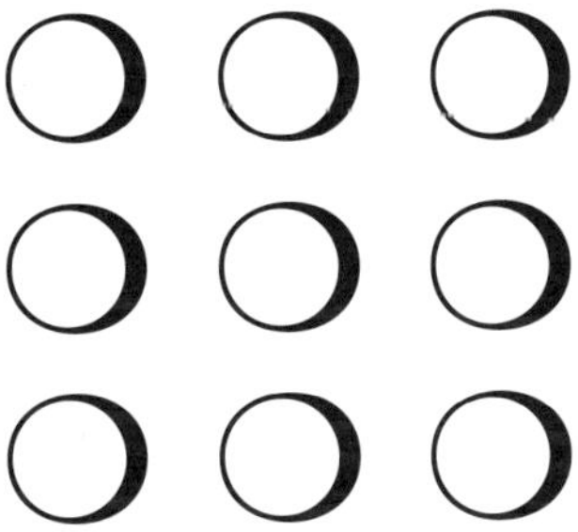
10 ten	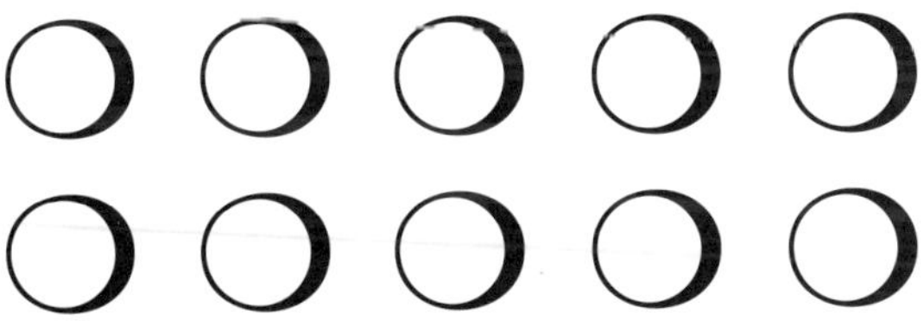

Name ______________________________

What I Feel and Hear

quiet	loud
wet	dry
hard	soft

Name ______________________________

Pictures to Describe

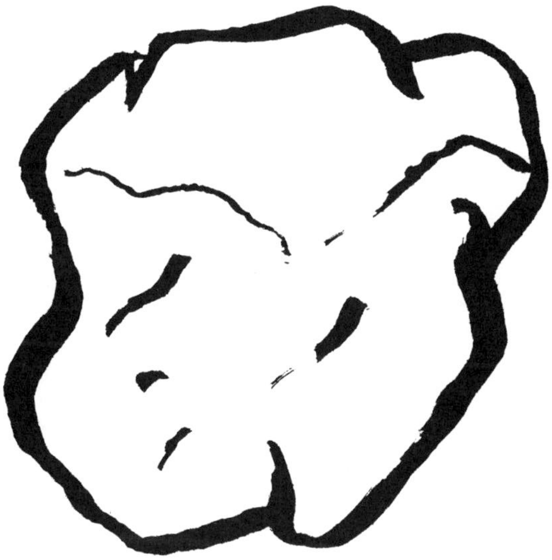

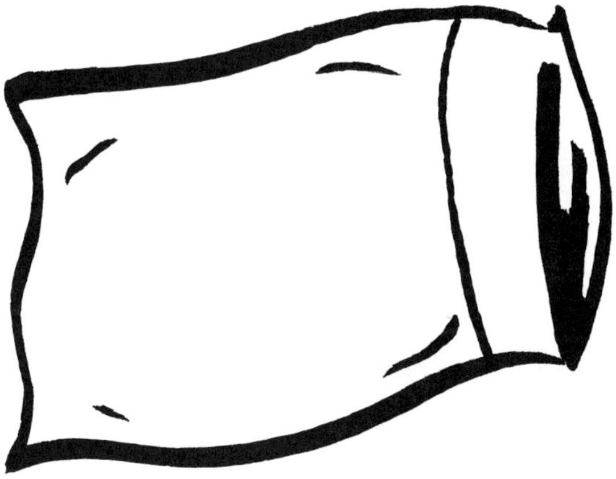

Have children identify the objects above (rock, pillow, ice cream cone, sun). Encourage them to use describing words to describe each object.

Name ____________________

My Favorite Food

I like to eat ____________________.

Name ______________________________

Smells So Good!

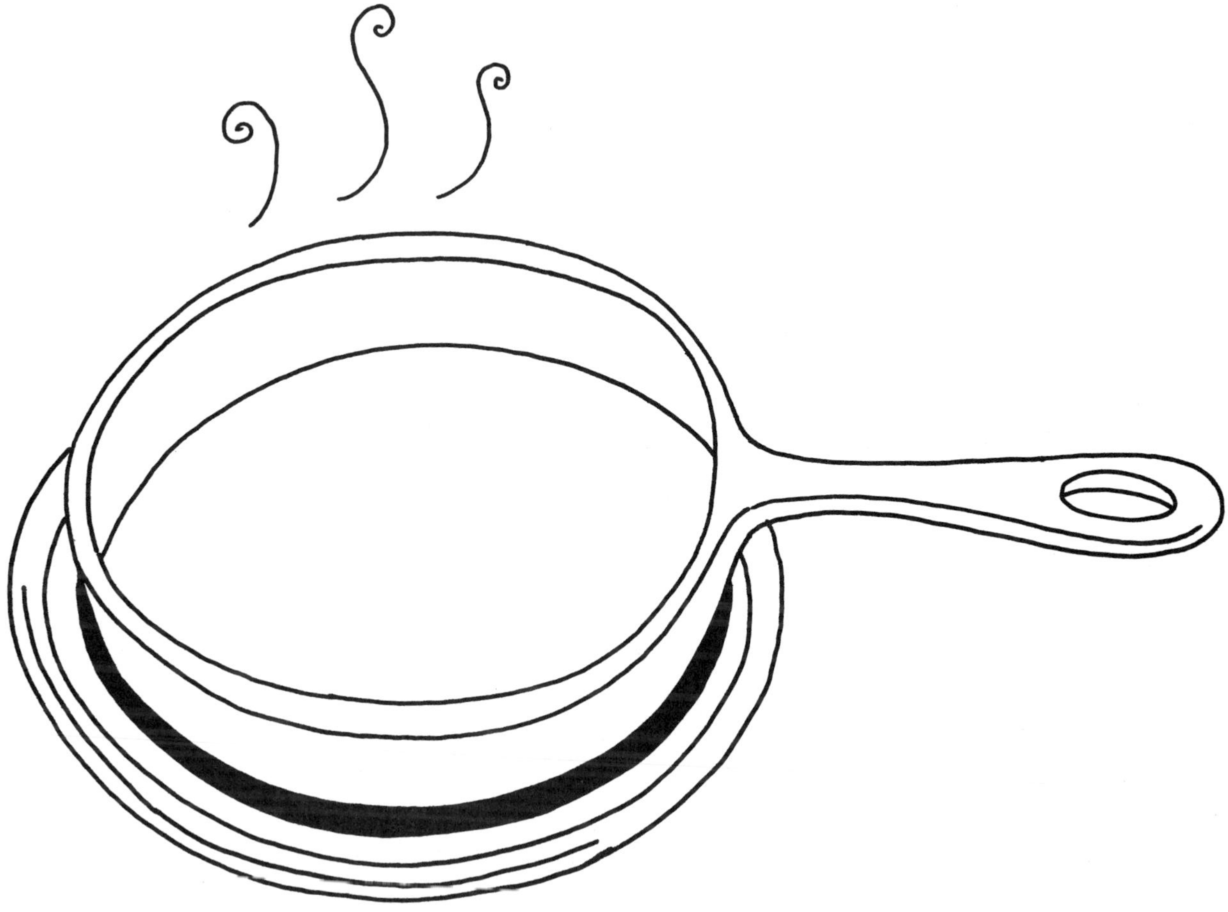

______________________________ smells so good.

Name ______________________________

What's the Order?

1.

	 eat pizza.

2.

	 digs.

3.

 The baby	

 The children	 The dog	 wants the toy.

Have children make complete sentences by cutting out the pictures at the bottom and glueing them into the matching box. Read the sentences together.

Name ______________________________

Sandwich Fixings

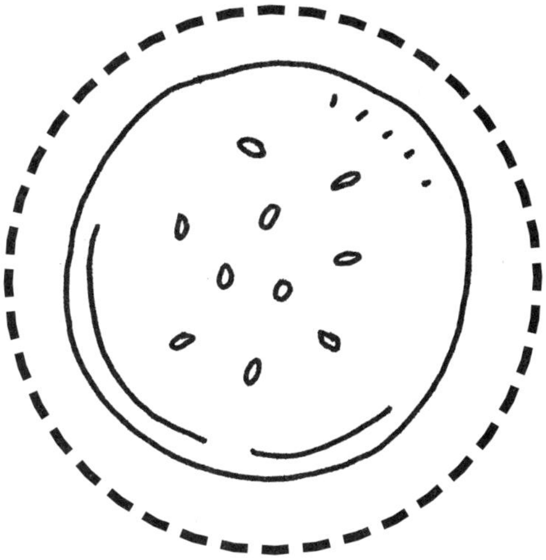

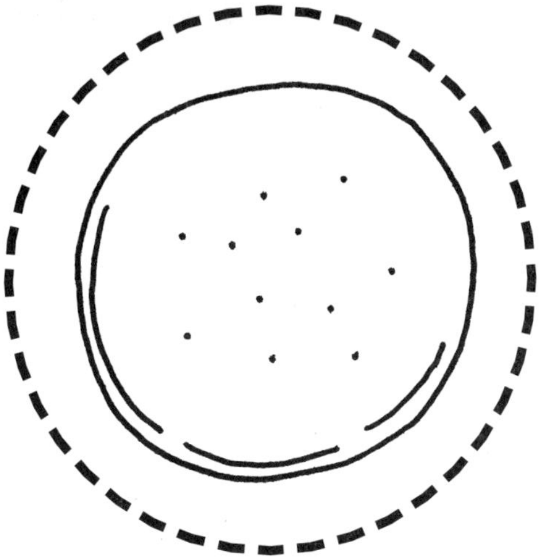

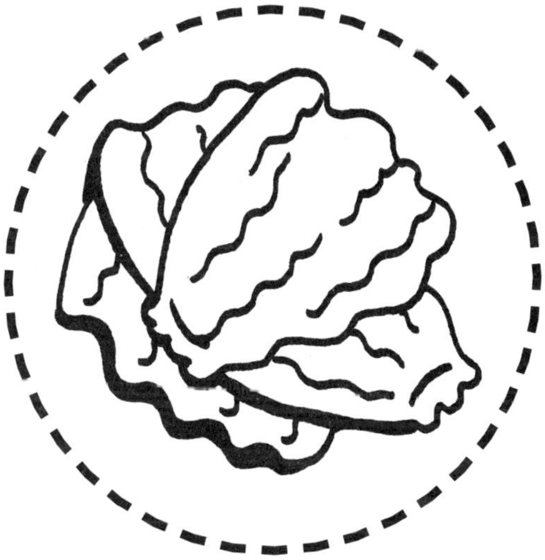

Have children cut out the pictures of buns, tomatoes, meat, lettuce, and cheese. Ask them to color them and then make a sandwich using the pictures. Encourage children to talk about the steps.

Name ____________________

"The Gingerbread Man" Cutout

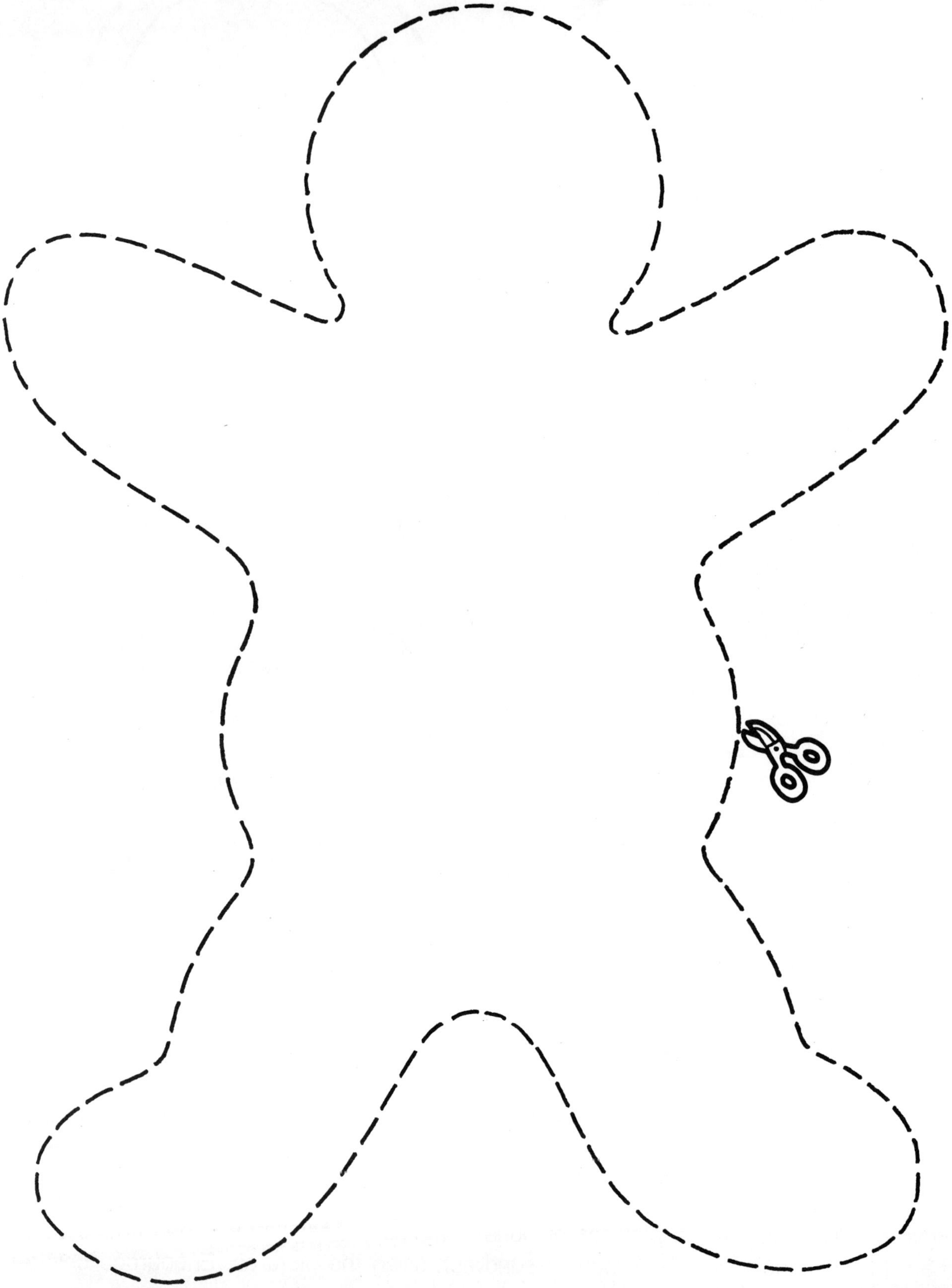

Name ______________________________

Mark My Words!

This is me!

Who are you?

Come and play.

Read the statements. Have children identify and circle the sentence end marks. Then have them draw a picture to illustrate the sentences.

Name ______________________________

My Favorite Character

____

Name ______________________________

MY STORY

Name ______________________________

"My Brown Bear Barney"

Have children cut out the characters and use them to retell the story.

Name ________________________________

"Pablo's Tree"

Have children color and cut out the tree and decorations. Ask children to retell the story using the tree decorations in the correct order.

Name ______________________________

"A Letter to Amy"

Have children discuss their favorite part of the story. Ask them to decorate a postage stamp with a picture from their favorite part. Invite children to discuss their favorite parts with a partner.

Name ____

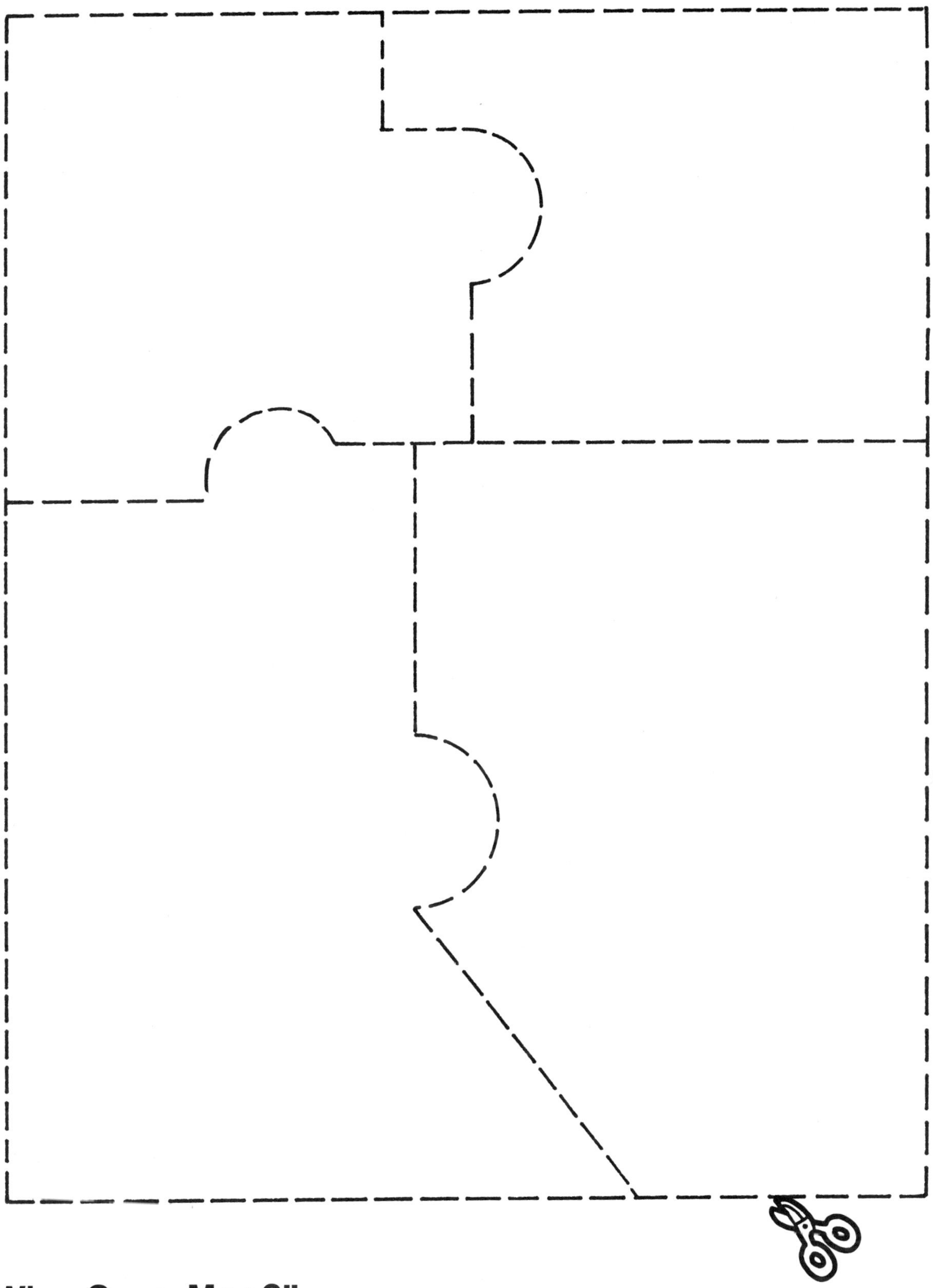

"Who Says Moo?"

Have children create their own animal puzzle by drawing an animal from the story onto the puzzle pieces. Have children share their puzzle with a partner.

Name ______________________________

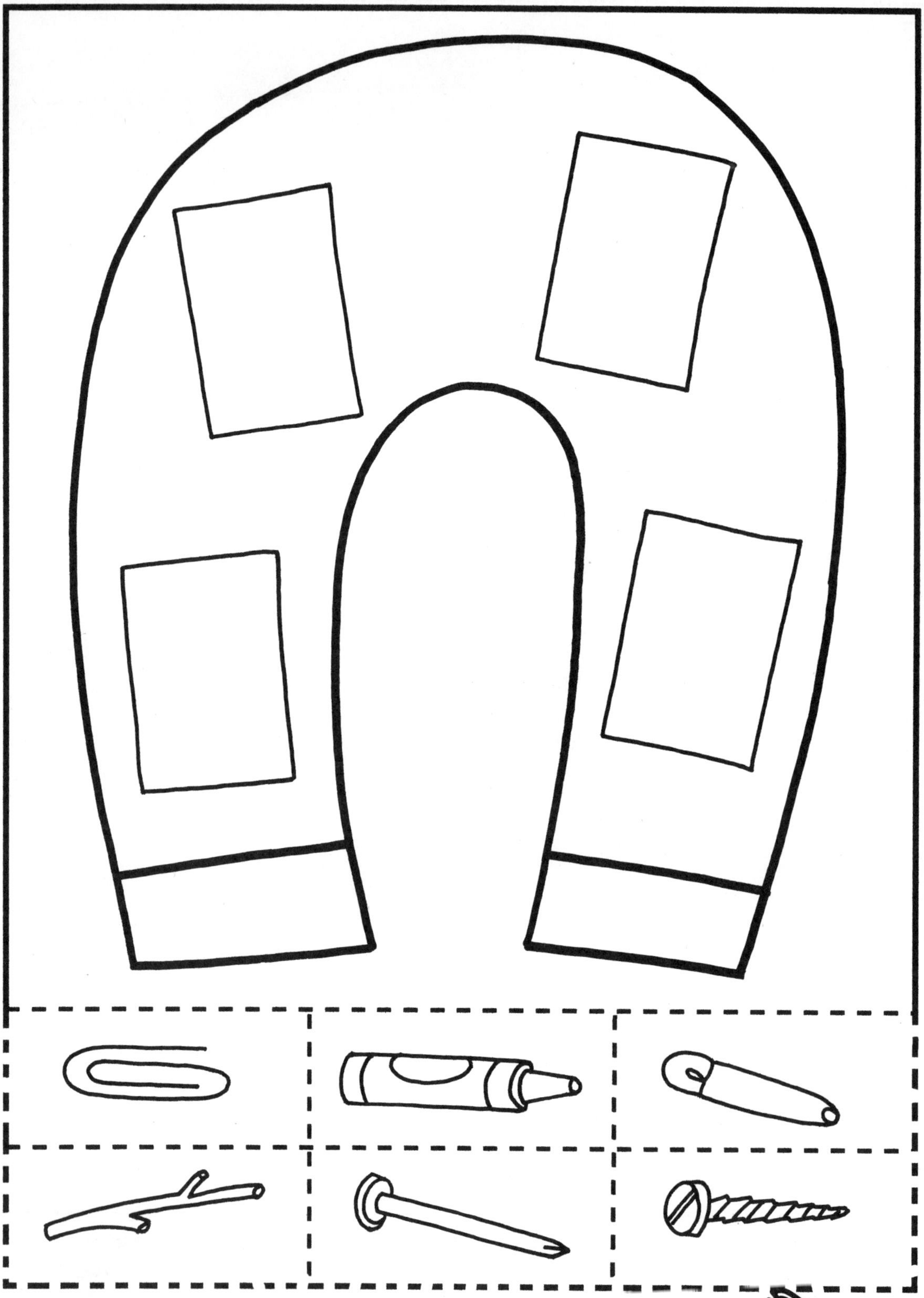

"What Makes a Magnet?"

Have children cut out the boxes and glue on the objects that the magnet picked up.

Name ______________________________

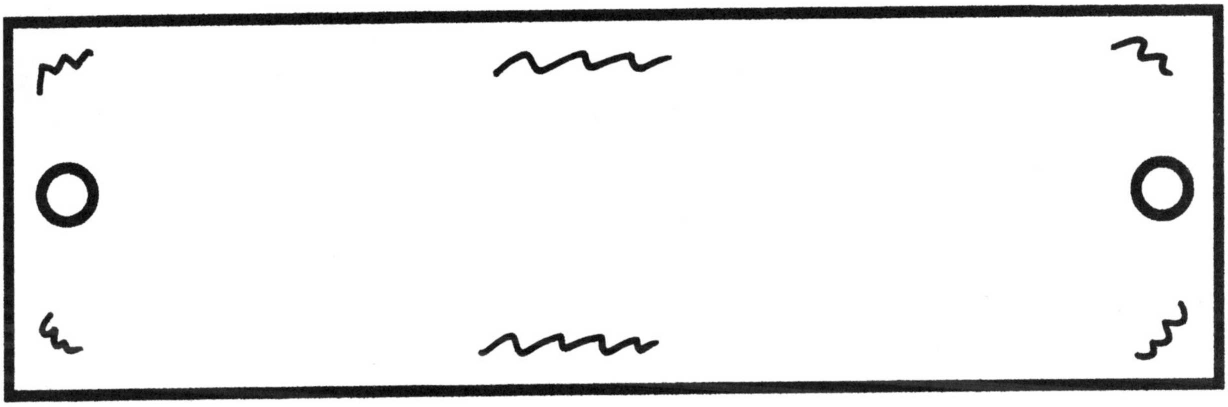

"Two of Everything"

Have children discuss what they would like to put in the pot. Ask them to draw it on the bracelet. Have them draw two of that object on the other bracelet, as if one were placed into the pot and came out as two. Invite children to share their bracelets with a classmate and to talk about them.

Name ______________________________

My Photo Album

______________________________ ______________________________

____

Name ______________________________

Story Web

Name ______________________________

Rules of the Game

Name ____

Animal Descriptions

Name ______________________________

How to Make a Handprint Paperweight

First

Next

Last

Name ______________________________

The Magic Pot

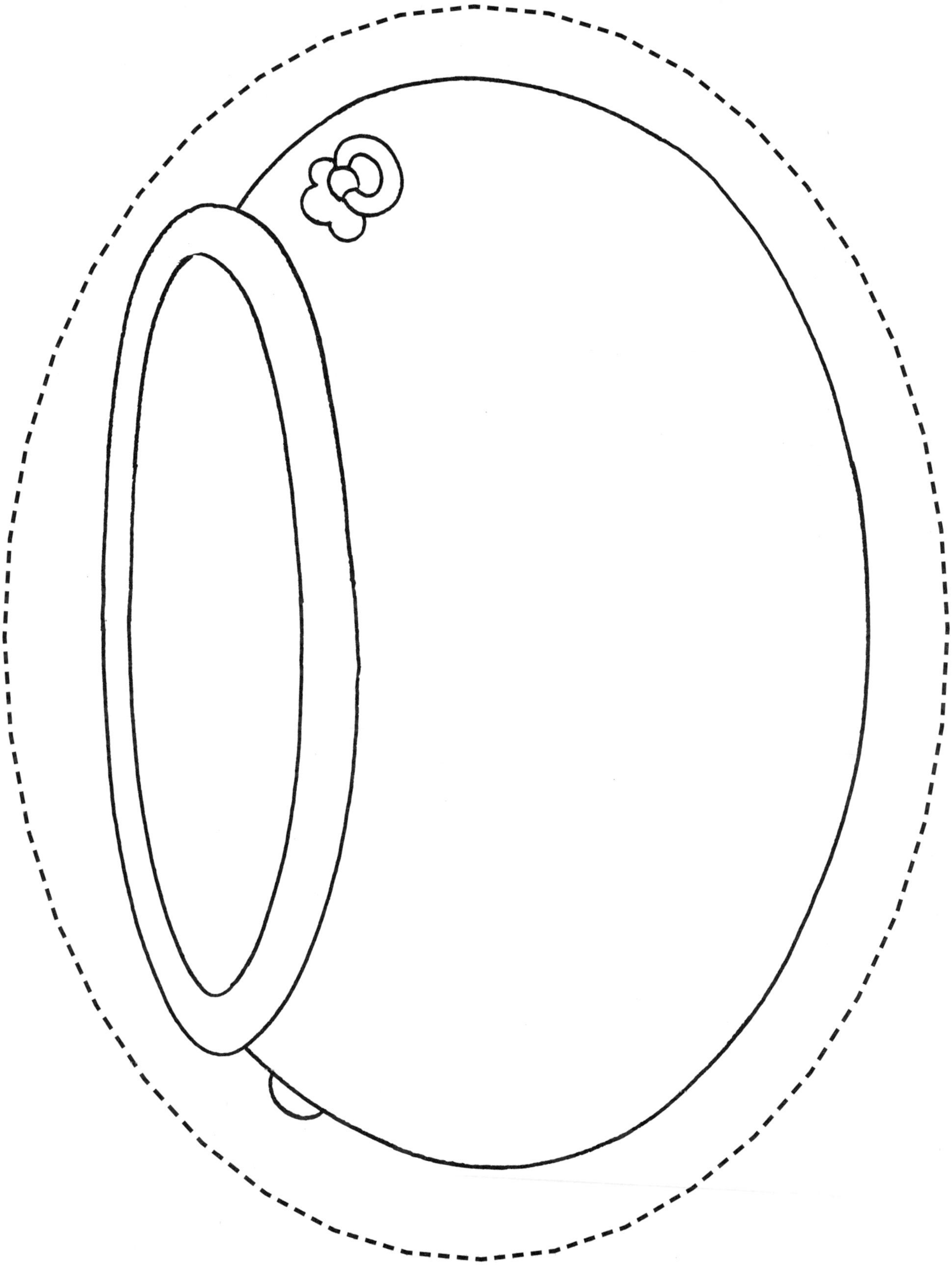

School-Home Connection

ABC and Me

Dear Family Members,

As your child begins kindergarten, we will be doing activities that help your child learn the letters of the alphabet, rhyming words, and new vocabulary. The unit culminates in a shared writing activity in which your child will help to write a class journal entry.

Books to Read

I Like Me! by Nancy Carlson. Viking, 1988.

Arthur's Family Vacation by Marc Brown. Little, Brown, 1994.

Chicka Chicka Boom Boom by Bill Martin, Jr. and John Archambault. Simon & Schuster, 1990.

HELPING YOUR CHILD LEARN

You can help reinforce the skills your child is learning at school. Here are some tips:

- Point out the letters that make up your child's name. Have your child practice writing his or her name.
- Sing songs and say nursery rhymes with your child.
- Talk with your child about his or her daily activities. Help your child use new or unusual words.

THEME ACTIVITIES

- **Play an animal alphabet game with your child.** Try to think of an animal for every letter of the alphabet: "A is for aardvark, B is for bat," and so on.
- **Look through a photo album.** Look through a photo album together with your child. Talk about the stages your child has gone through from baby to the present. Discuss things your child can do now that he or she couldn't do before.
- **Find some interesting pictures in a magazine.** Describe all the details that you both see. Use new and unusual words in your descriptions.

School-Home Connection

Family, Friends, and Fun

Books to Read

The Beautiful Butterfly: A Folktale From Spain by Judy Sierra. Clarion, 2000.

Dogs Don't Wear Sneakers by Laura Numeroff. Simon & Schuster, 1994.

How Do You Say It Today, Jessie Bear? by Nancy White Carlstrom, 1993.

Dear Family Members,

In this theme, *Family, Friends, and Fun,* your child is going to learn about naming words for people and things; special names, such as holiday names and days of the week; and plural names for more than one. The unit culminates in an interactive writing activity in which your child will help to write a personal story.

HELPING YOUR CHILD LEARN

You can help reinforce the skills your child is learning at school. Here are some tips:

- While driving in the car or shopping in a store, name the things that you both see.
- Talk with your child about the days of the week. For example, ask "What day is today?" "What day was yesterday?" "What day will it be tomorrow?"
- Ask your child to tell about his or her favorite holidays.

THEME ACTIVITIES

- **Play a game of "I Spy";** for example, say "I spy a tall, brown object with green leaves. What is it?" Have your child guess the mystery object. Then switch roles.
- **Look through a calendar with your child.** Name the months together. Then help your child name the major holidays and the months in which they occur.
- **Look around the house together for items of which there are more than one.** Take turns naming what you see; for example, "I see four towels," "I see three potatoes," and so on.

School-Home Connection

What Shall We Do?

Dear Family Members,

In this theme, *What Shall We Do?*, your child is going to learn about action words and following directions. The unit culminates in an interactive writing activity in which your child will help to write an invitation.

Books to Read

Benjamin Bigfoot by Mary Serfozo. Margaret McElderry, 1993.

Dad's Dinosaur Day by Diane Dawson Hearn. Simon & Schuster, 1993.

School Bus: For the Buses, the Riders, and the Watchers by Donald Crews. Mulberry Books, 1993.

HELPING YOUR CHILD LEARN

You can help reinforce the skills your child is learning at school. Here are some tips:

- Read a story to your child. Then listen as your child tells you about the actions that happened in the story.
- Talk with your child about his or her favorite outdoor games.
- Have your child help you follow directions while you cook.

THEME ACTIVITIES

- **Play an action word game where you and your child take turns saying sentences like these:** "I can run like a cheetah," "I can swim like a fish," and so on.
- **Provide crayons and paper.** Encourage your child to draw his or her favorite school activities. Then listen as he or she describes them.
- **Play a funny game in which your child has to follow directions.** For example, say "First, bring me the book. Then hop up and down three times." Then switch roles.

School-Home Connection

Color Your World

Dear Family Members,

In this theme, your child is going to learn about describing words for colors, shapes, and numbers. Your child will also learn about the five senses. The unit culminates in an interactive writing activity in which your child will help write an animal description.

Books to Read

Everett Anderson's 1-2-3 by Lucille Clifton. Henry Holt & Company, Inc., 1992.

Green Wilma by Tedd Arnold. Dial, 1994.

Little Grunt and the Big Egg: A Prehistoric Fairy Tale by Tomie dePaola. Holiday House, 1990.

HELPING YOUR CHILD LEARN

You can help your child learn and practice his or her colors, numbers, and shapes at home. Here are some tips:

- Point out objects by color when you and your child are together; for example, "Look at the blue car," "Do you see the red bird?" and so on.
- Count with your child as you do everyday tasks; for example, "How many forks are on the table?" "How many apples did we buy?" and so on.
- Point out objects by shape when you and your child are together; for example, "Would you like a round orange?" "Please hand me the square box." and so on.

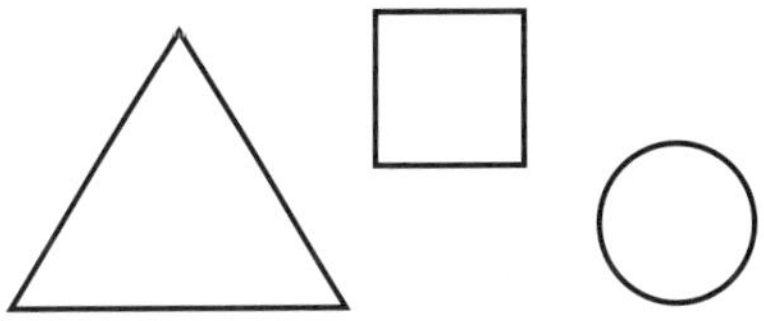

THEME ACTIVITIES

- **Go on a "color hunt" with your child.** Look together for as many red (blue, green, yellow, purple) items as you can.
- **Play a counting game while you are driving with your child.** Have your child count the number of stop signs you pass. He or she can also read aloud the numbers found on road and store signs.
- **Go on a "shape hunt" with your child.** Look together for circles, squares, and triangles in and around your home.

School-Home Connection

Follow Me

Dear Family Members,

In this theme, *Follow Me,* your child is going to learn about words and sentences, capital letters, and sequence words. The unit culminates in an interactive writing activity in which your child will help to write a class how-to that tells how to do or make something.

Books to Read

Grandpa's Soup by Eiko Kadono. Eerdmans Publishing Company, 1999.

Is Your Mama a Llama? by Deborah Guarino. Scholastic, 1990.

Max's Breakfast by Rosemary Wells. Dila, 1998.

HELPING YOUR CHILD LEARN

You can help reinforce the skills your child is learning at school. Here are some tips:

- When reading with your child, ask him or her to show you the difference between letters and words.
- When driving in the car or shopping in a store, search together for capital and lowercase letters.
- Read a story to your child. Talk together about what happened first, next, and last in the story.

THEME ACTIVITIES

- **Play a game where your child has to finish a sentence that you begin;** for example, "I like to play ______," "For dinner, I would like to eat ______," and so on.
- **Write a list of your family members' names.** Ask your child to find and name all of the capital letters.
- **Provide the ingredients for a sandwich.** Ask your child to give you directions for how to make the sandwich. Then eat it together!

School-Home Connection

Once Upon a Time

Dear Family Members,

In this theme, *Once Upon a Time,* your child will learn about different kinds of sentences—those that tell and those that ask. Your child will also learn about the elements that make up a story—character, setting, beginning, and end. The unit culminates in an interactive writing activity in which your child will help to write a story.

Books to Read

Aunt Isabel Tells a Good One by Kate Duke. Dutton, 1992.

Cinderella Penguin retold by Janet Perlman. Viking, 1994.

Special People, Special Ways by Arlene Maguire. Portunus Publishing Co., 1999.

HELPING YOUR CHILD LEARN

You can help reinforce the skills your child is learning at school. Here are some tips:

- Read a story to your child. Ask questions about what happened in the story.
- Ask your child to recall characters from stories you have read together in the past; for example, "Who was the character who wore a red cape and went to see her grandmother?"
- Talk with your child about what happens at the beginning, middle, and end of a typical day.

THEME ACTIVITIES

- **Take turns asking and answering questions with your child;** for example, ask "What is your favorite food?" "What color are your shoes?" and so on.
- **Provide crayons and paper.** Ask your child to draw what happens at the beginning, middle, and end of a school day. Listen as your child describes the drawings.
- **Act out a favorite story or fairy tale together,** such as "Red Riding Hood," "The Three Bears," or "The Three Little Pigs." Make simple costumes.

Name ______________________________

Letter Cards (Lowercase)

a	b	c	d	e
f	g	h	i	j
k	l	m	n	o
p	q	r	s	t
u	v	w	x	y
z				

Name ______________________________

Letter Cards (Capital)

A	B	C	D	E
F	G	H	I	J
K	L	M	N	O
P	Q	R	S	T
U	V	W	X	Y
Z				

Name ______________________________

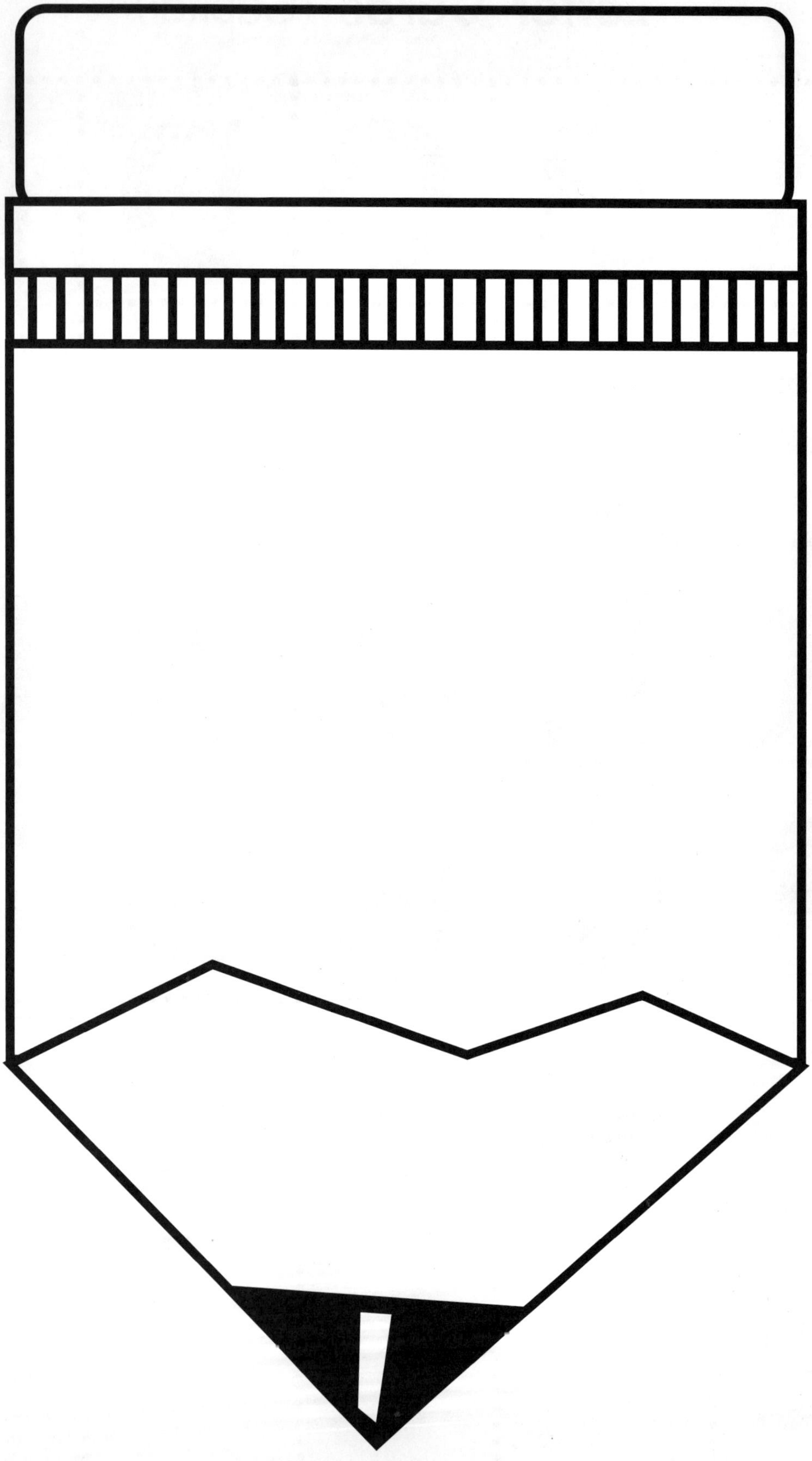

Name ____________________

Name ______________________________

Name ____

Name ____

Loop Game Board

Name ______________________________

Racetrack Game Board

1. Make two copies. 2. Cut out. 3. Glue onto a file folder.

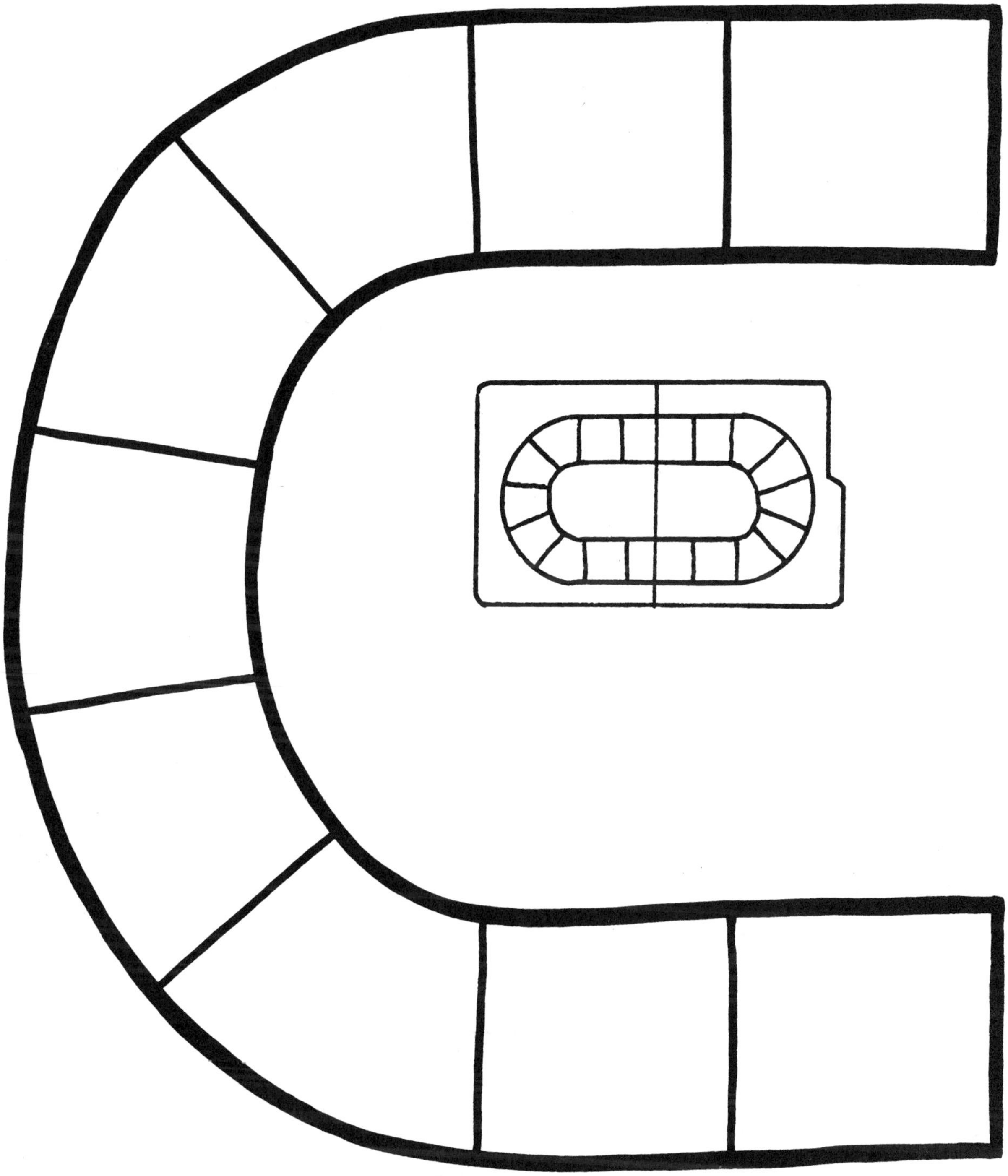

Name ______________________________

16-Square Grid

Name ____________________

S-Shape Game Board

1. Make two copies. 2. Cut out. 3. Glue onto a file folder.

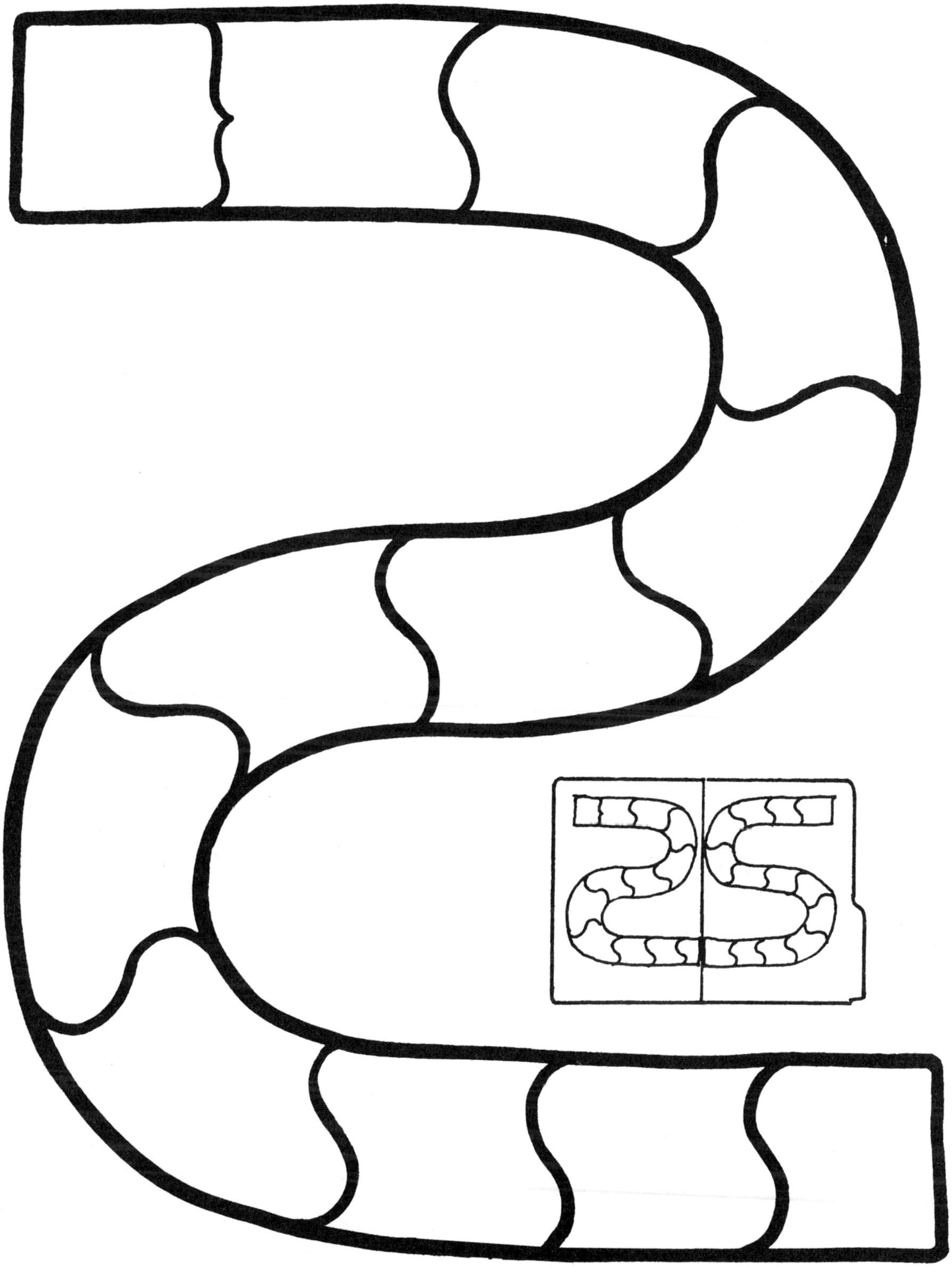

Name ______________________________

Concentration Cards

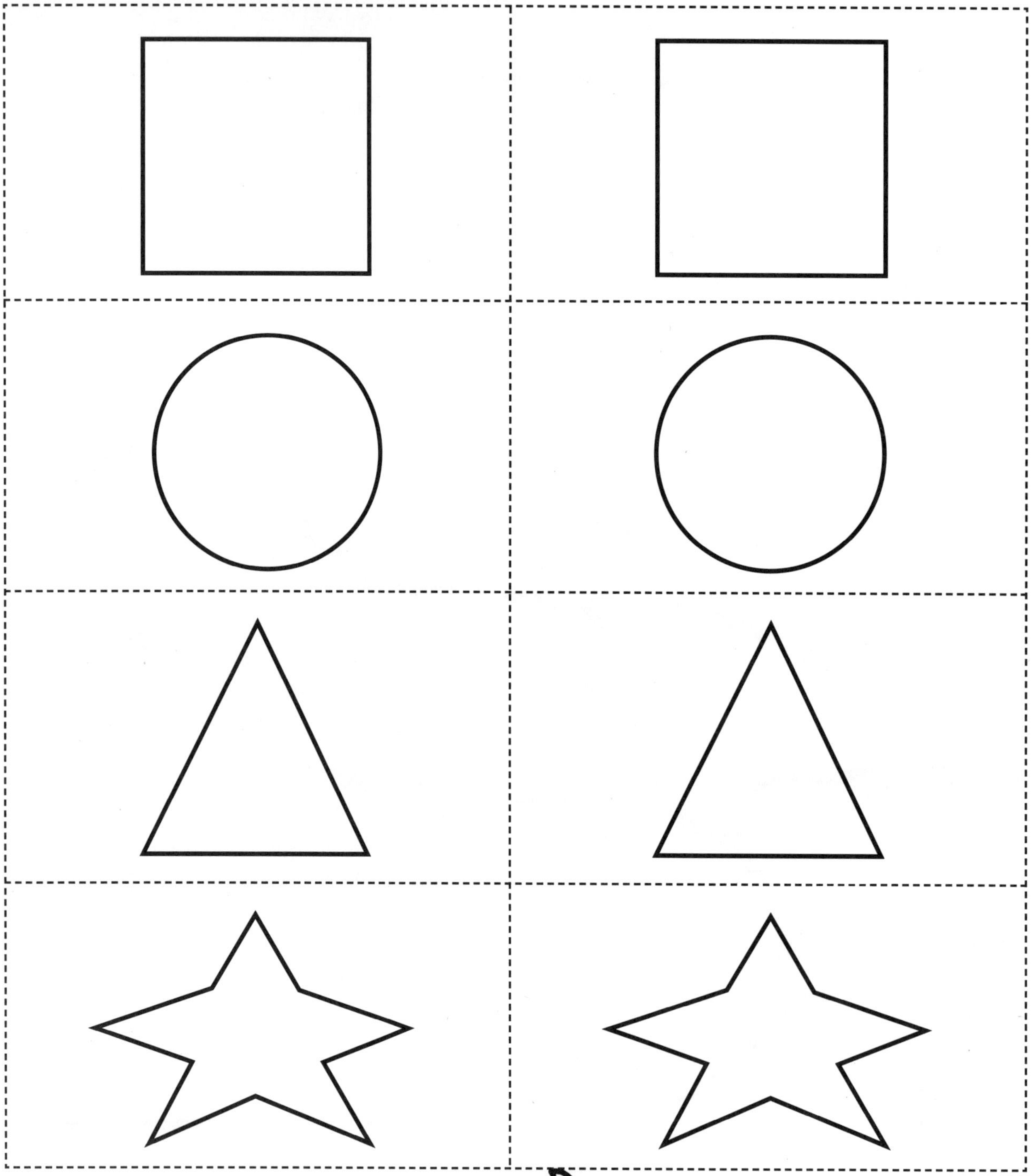

1. Have children cut out the cards.
2. Ask them to color the matching shapes the same color.
3. Children play "concentration" with a partner.

Name ______________________________

Castle Game Board

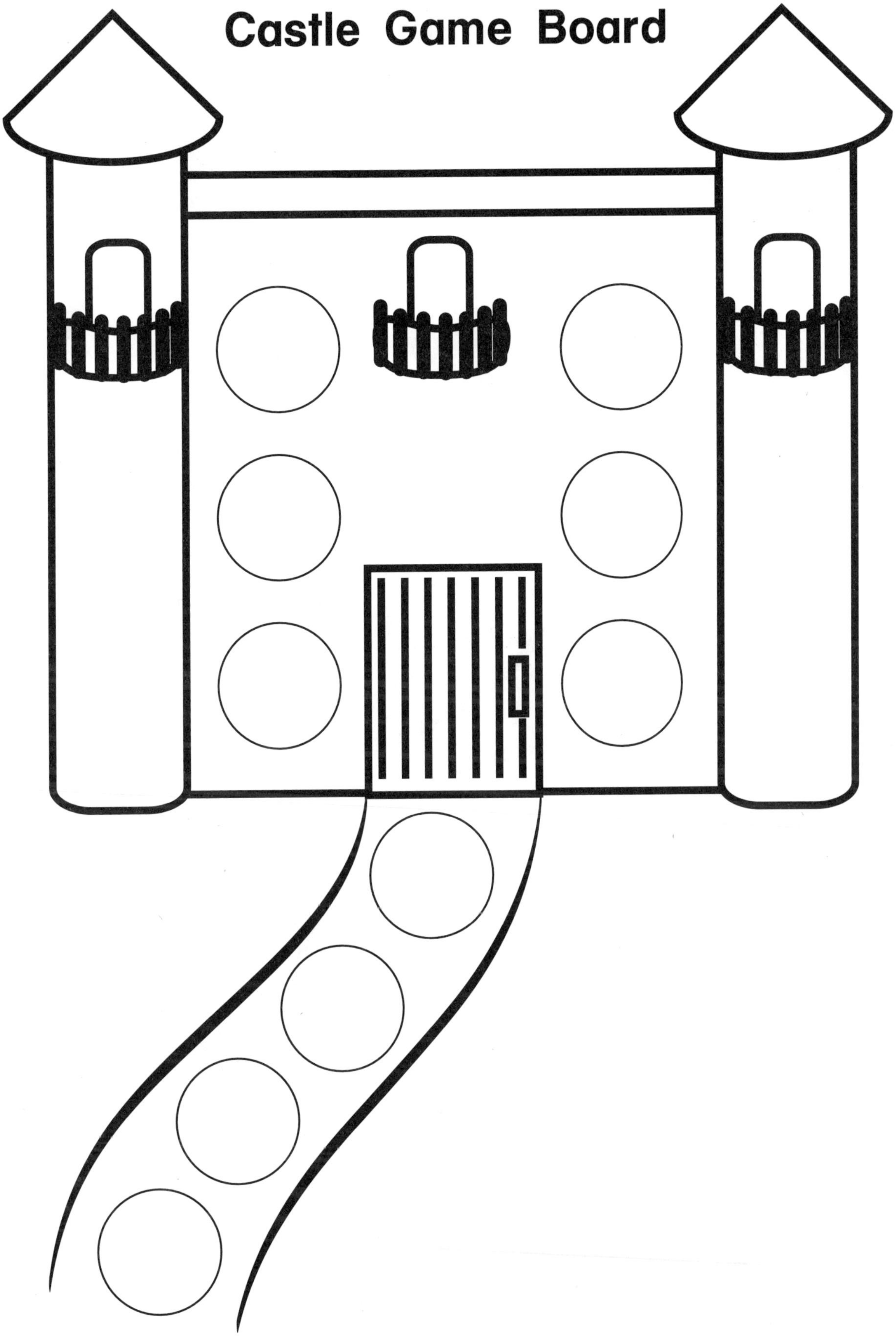

Name ______________________________

Spinners

1. Cut out a wheel and glue it onto thick paper.
2. Put on a paper clip with a brad.

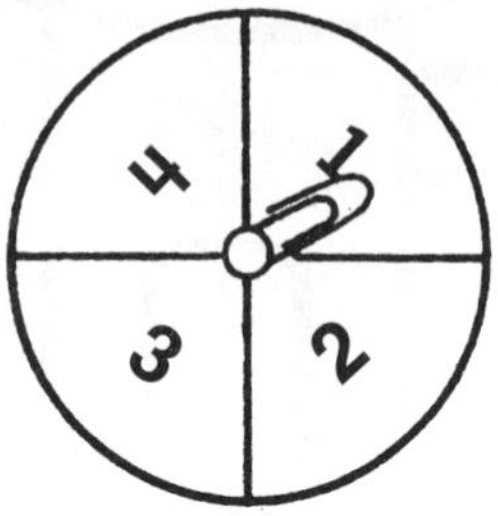

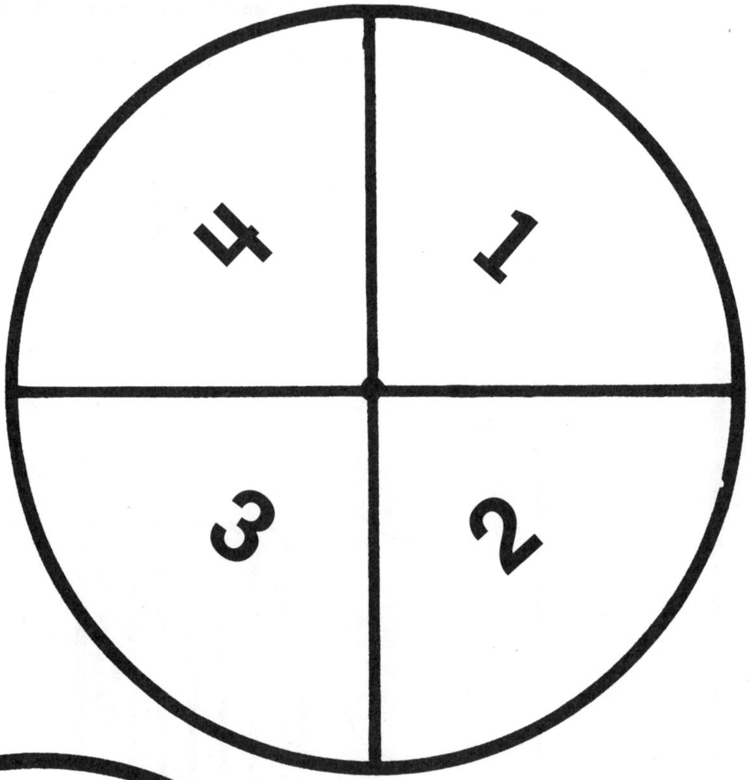

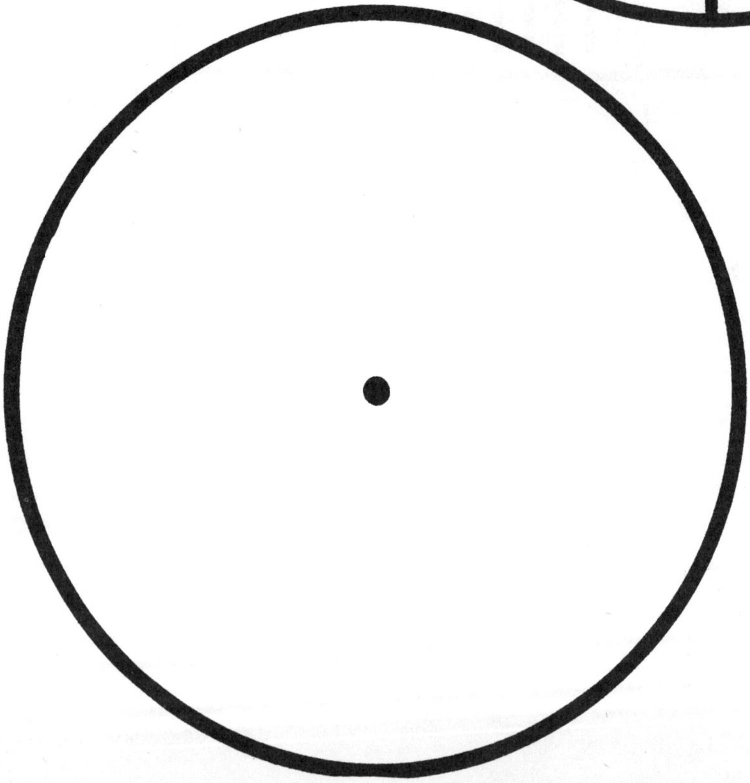

Blank Spinner

Name ______________________________

Pinwheel

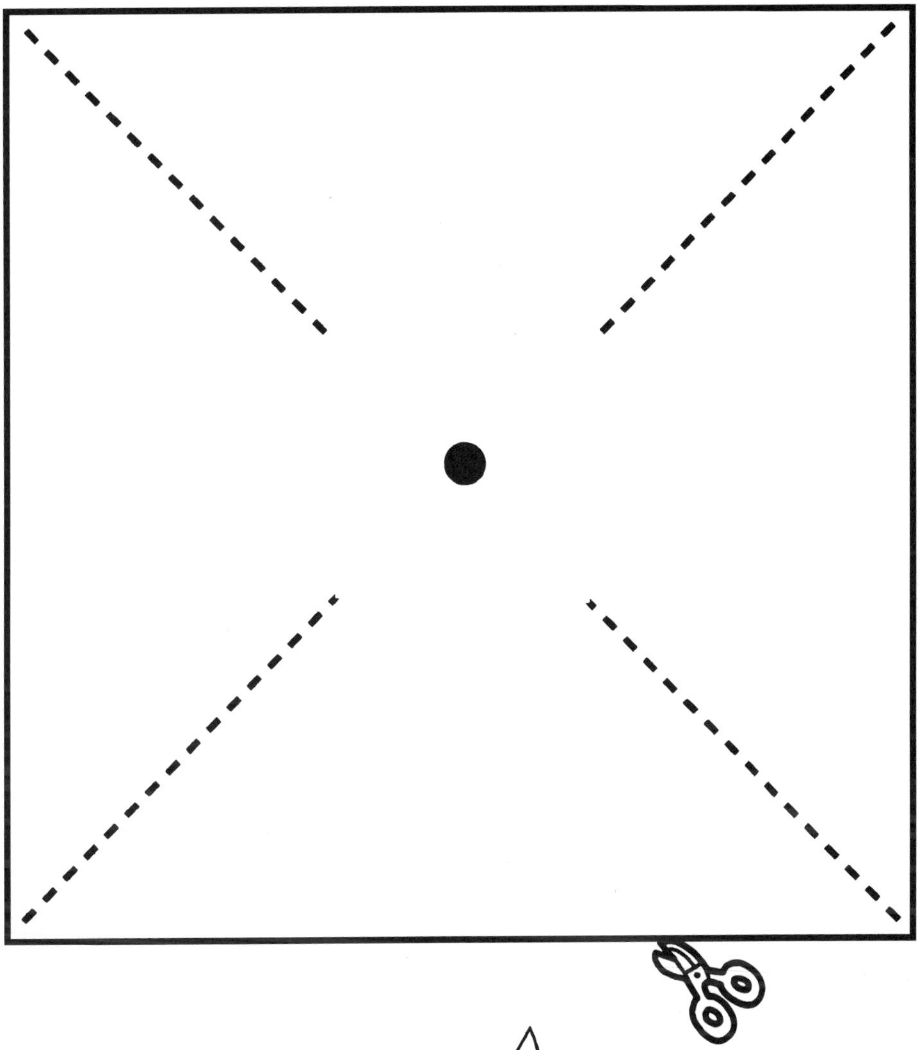

1. Cut out the pinwheel.
2. Bring each corner to the center and place a straight pin through it.
3. Push the pin through a straw.
4. Cover the end of the pin with tape.

Have children practice color or number words while playing with the pinwheel. Write each word on individual parts of the pinwheel.

Name ______________________________

Sun Visor

Have children make sun visors to use when discussing a weather theme.

1. Cut out sun visor pattern.

2. Punch out holes.

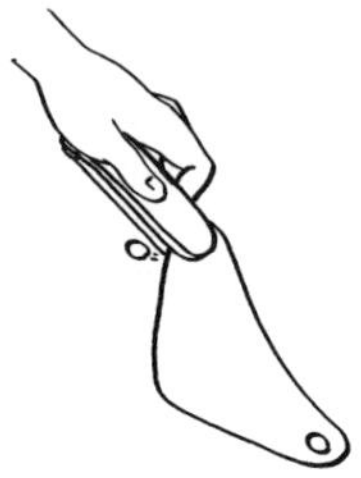

3. Attach string to each end of visor.

4. Decorate visor.

Name ______________________________

Award Pattern

Name ____________________

Paper-Plate Puppets

Make multiple copies of this sheet, or have children trace the puppet pieces. Have children glue the parts onto small paper plates to make different animals. Tape a large craft stick to the back. Children can use the puppets to retell stories or create new stories.

Name ____________________

"Me" Pattern

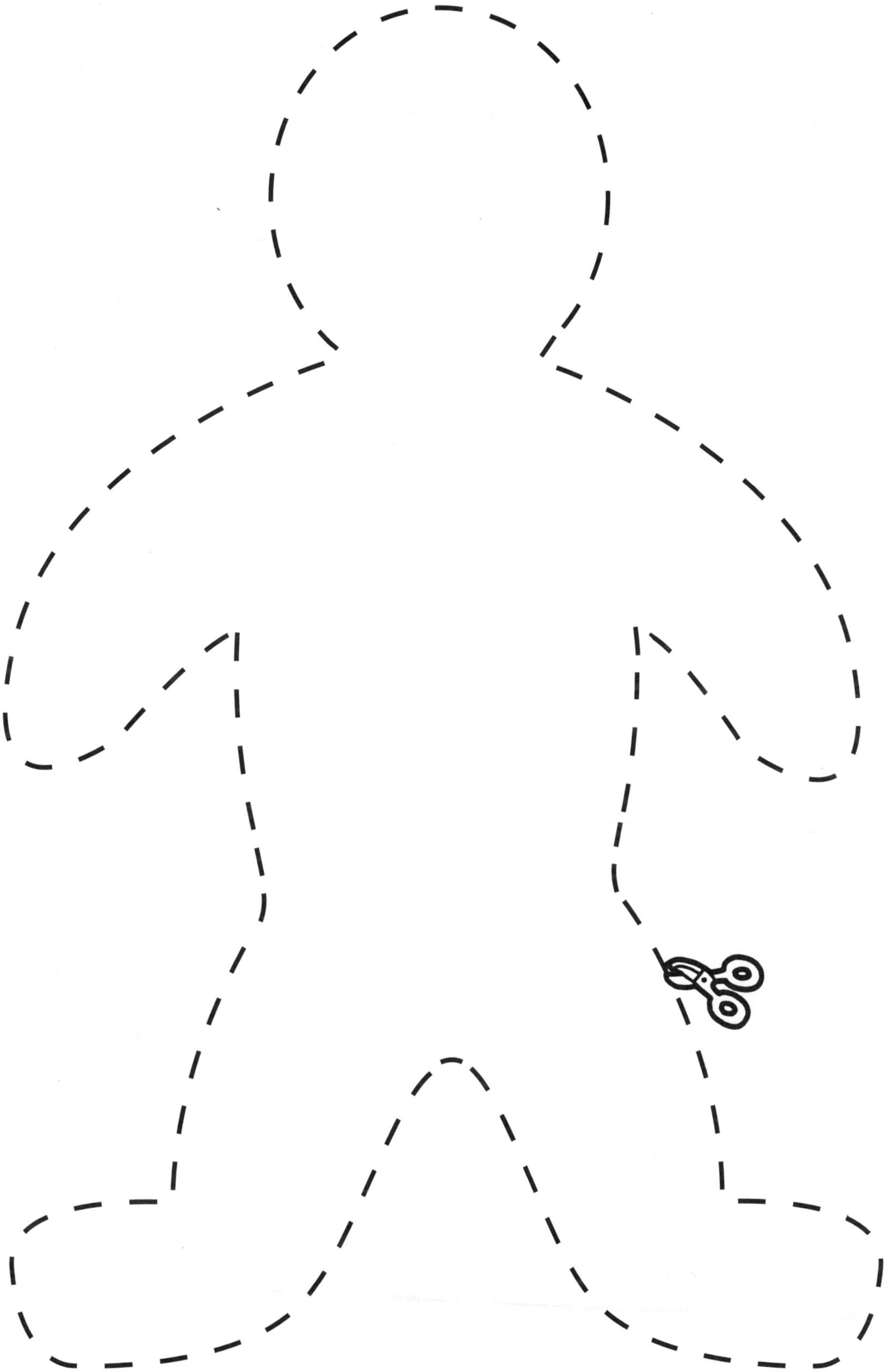

Name ______________________________

Stand-Up Book

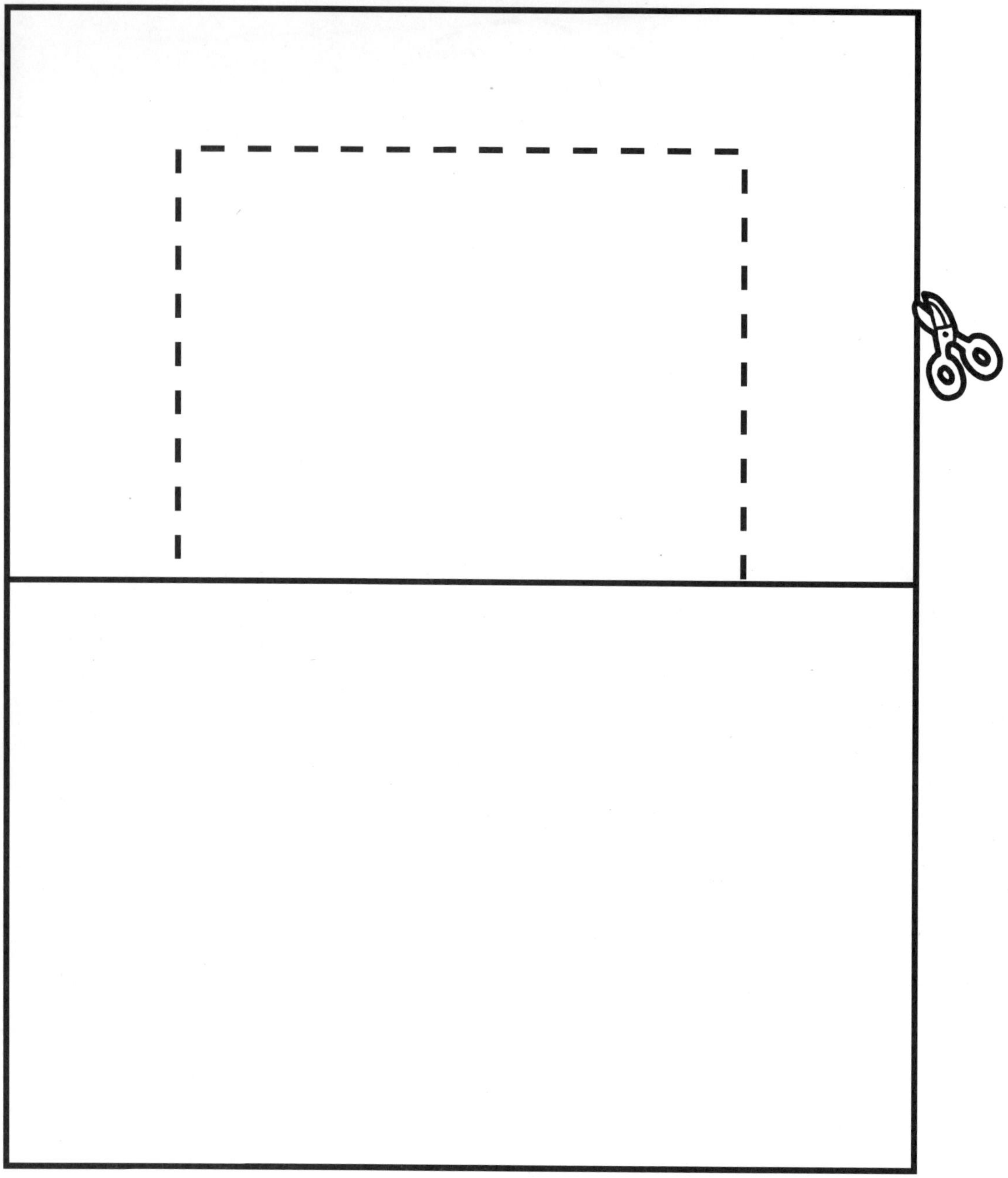

Have children make a stand-up book to publish a poem. Copy the poem or glue a poem onto the bottom half of the pattern. Draw a picture to accompany the poem within the dotted lines on the top half. Cut along the dotted lines and fold back the cut-out border to make the picture and poem stand.

Name ____________________

Pop-Up Card

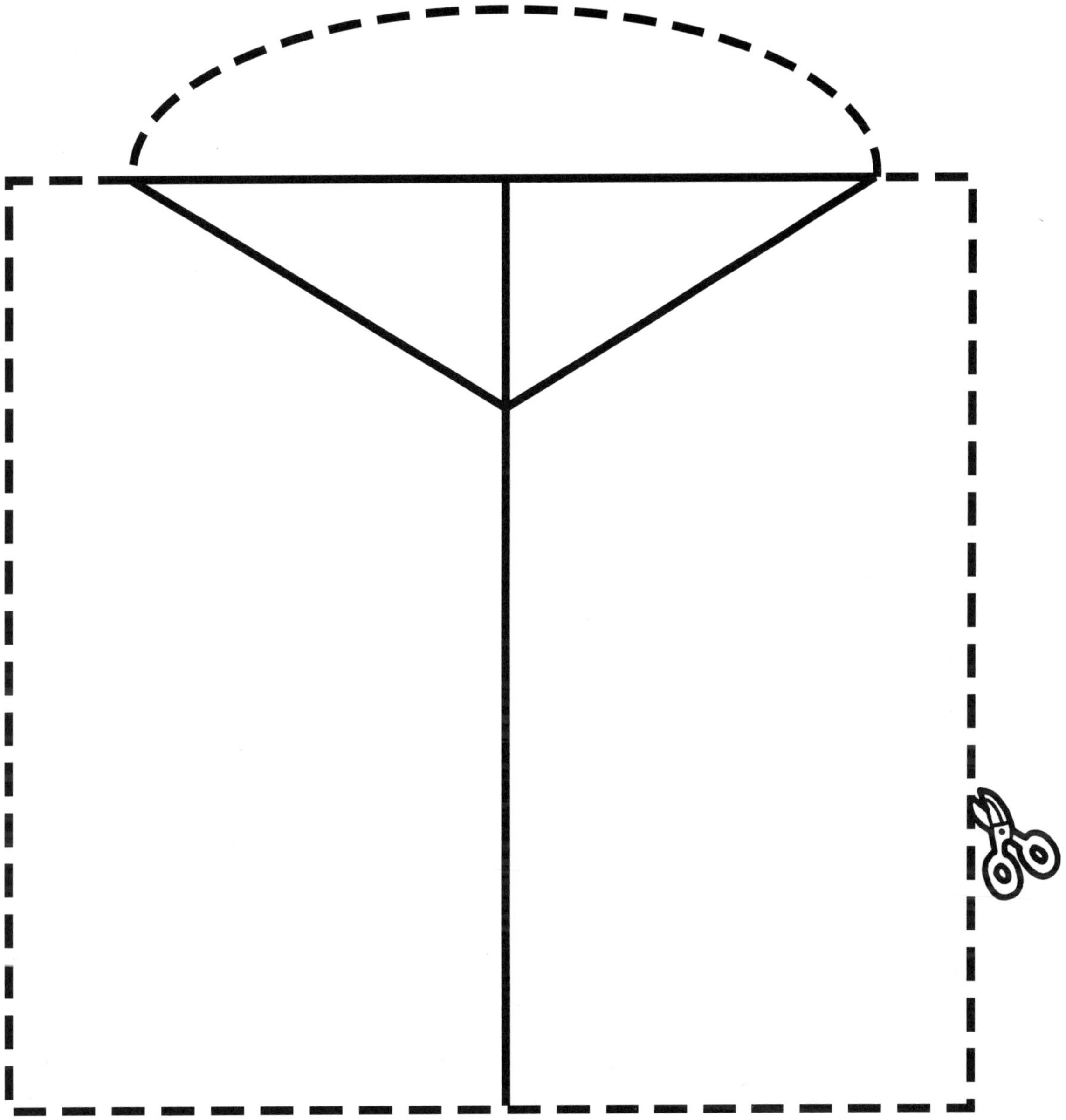

Have children cut out the pop-up card. Then have them fold the card on the solid lines. The pop-up area needs to be folded toward the inside of the card.

Name ______________________________

Flip Book

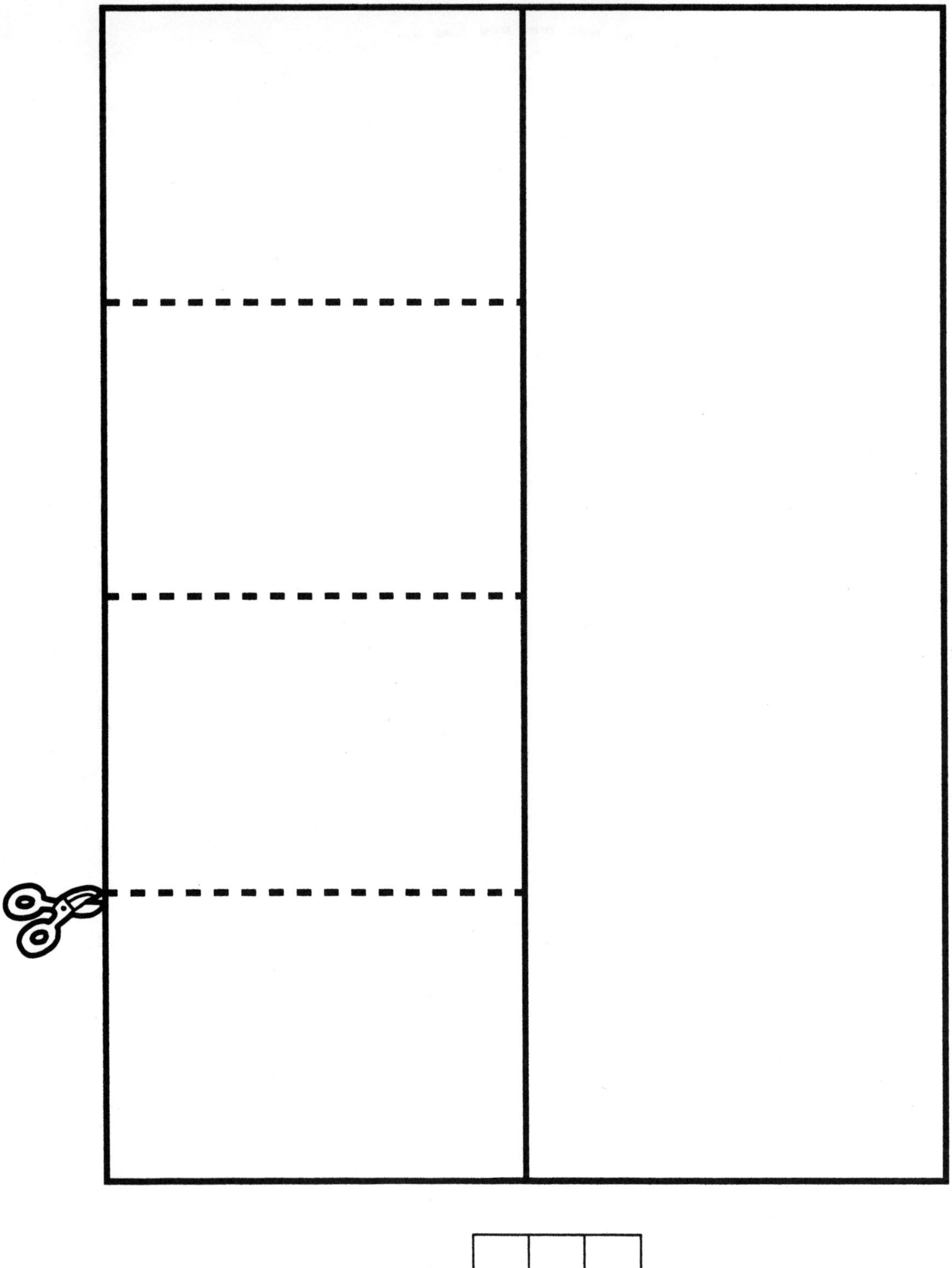

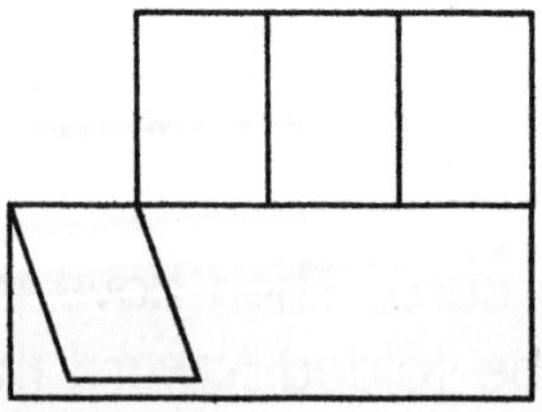

Name ______________________________

Family Tree Pattern

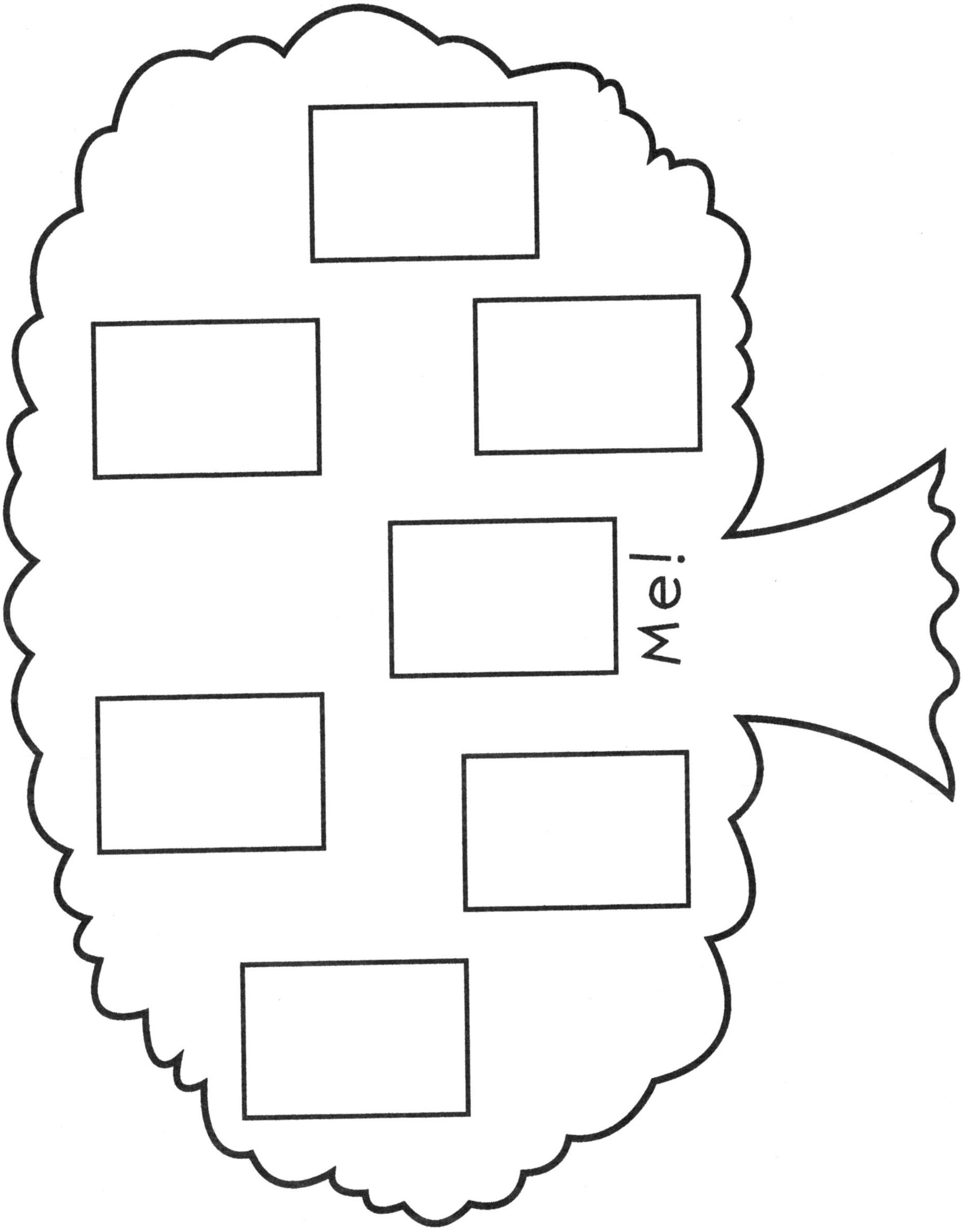

Have children draw seven members of their family in the tree. Make sure each child draws a picture of him- or herself in the center box.

Name ____________________

Recipe Card

Name ______________________________

Stand-Up Stage

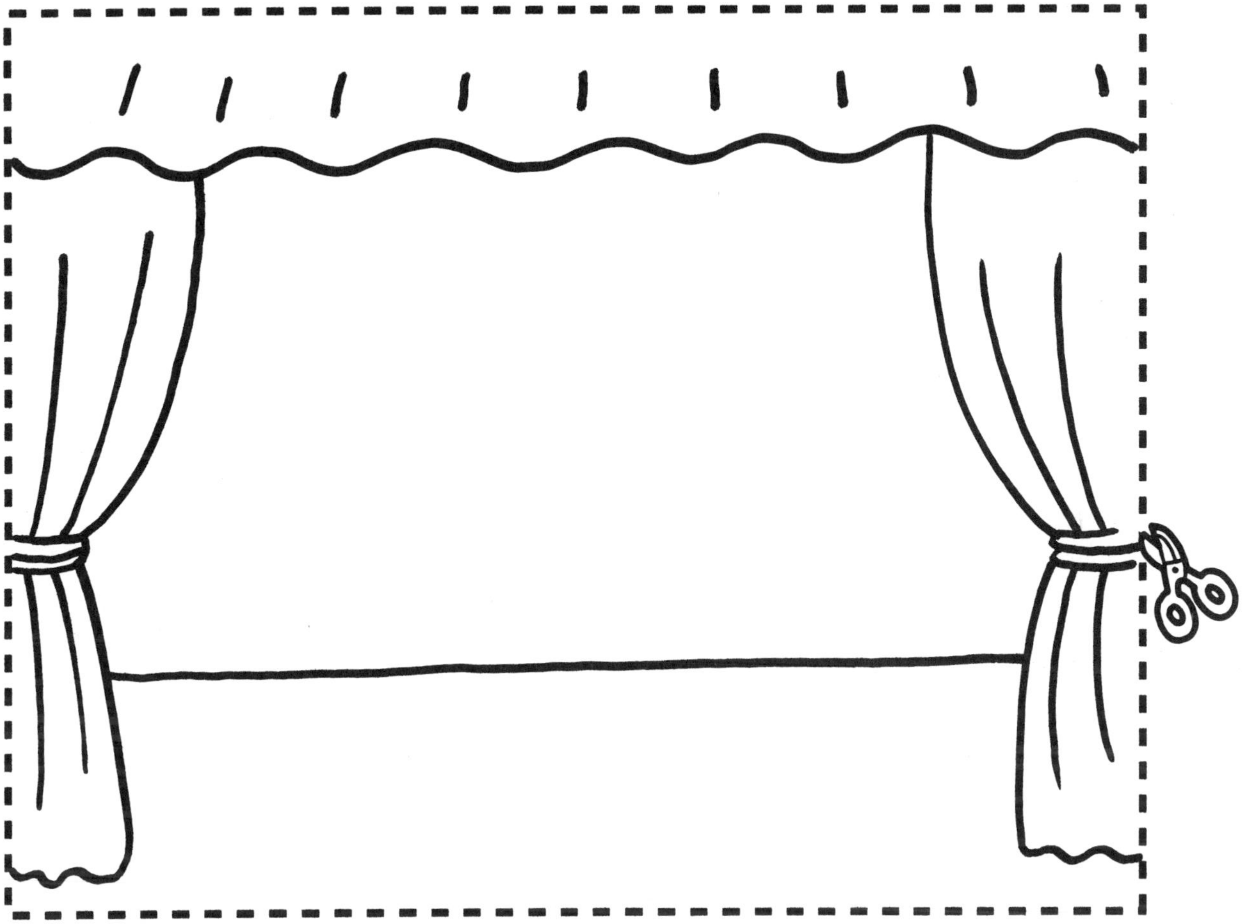

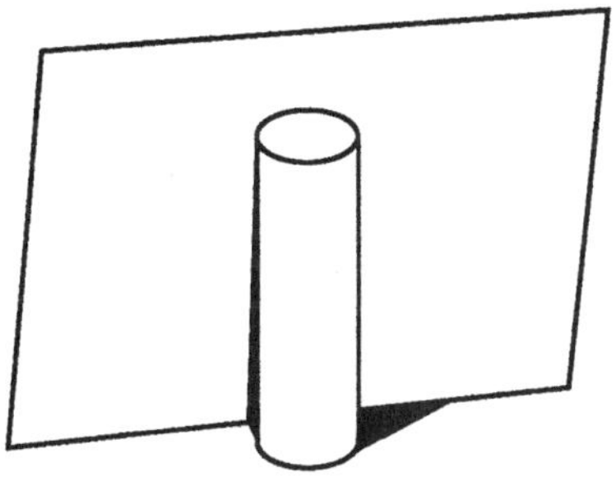

Have children cut out and color the stage. Attach a short cardboard tube to the back to make it stand. Use with finger puppets when telling or retelling a story.

Name ______________________________

Animal Finger Puppets

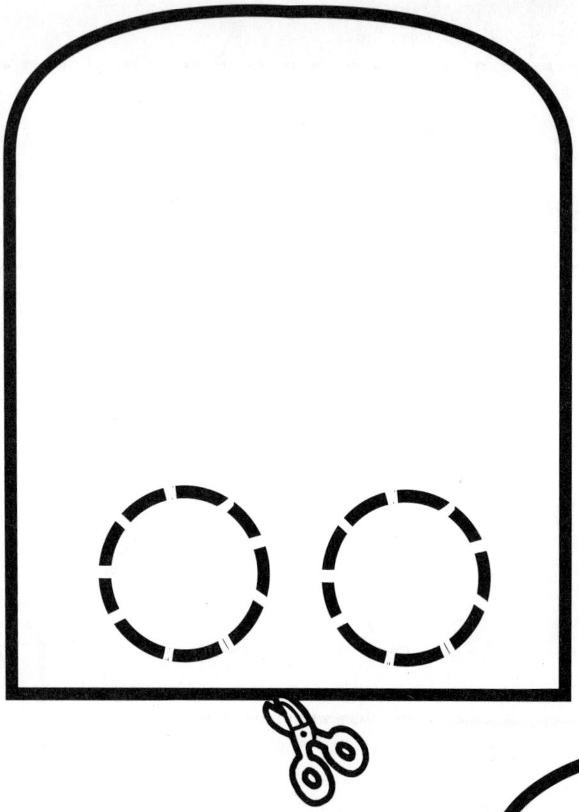

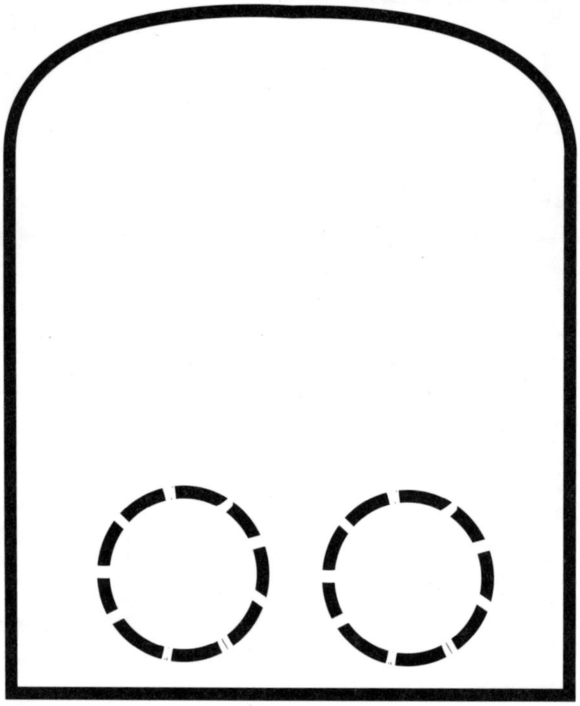

1. Draw. 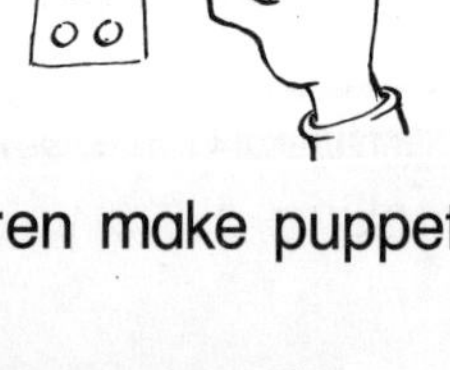 2. Cut. 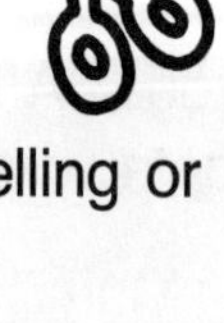 3. Have fun! 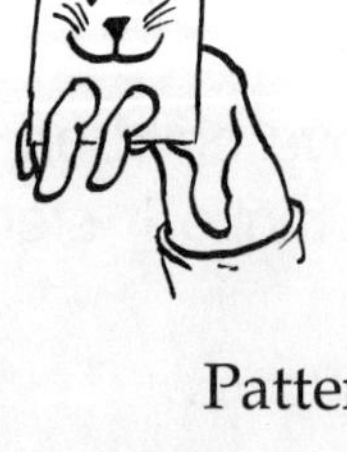

Have children make puppets to use in telling or retelling a story.